PRAISE FOR JE

"Zach Maldonado is an important voice to this generation of believers. Here, Zach shows us why we can trust the Jesus of the Bible and why He's better than religion, sin, and self-help. Get this book to be strengthened in your understanding and encouraged by your God."

—Andrew Farley
Pastor, national radio host, and bestselling author of *The Naked Gospel*

"Zach Maldonado has written a powerful, beautiful, poetic, and energetic book about how Jesus is better! Throughout, he points us to the One who is worthy of our praise. But not in some sentimental way. The worship of this God turns our life upside down—it's subversive! So beautiful. Go get this and read it time and again."

—Dr. A.J. Swoboda
Assistant professor of Bible and Christianity at Bushnell University and author of *After Doubt*.

"Zach is passionate about Jesus, and it shows. This book is a relentless, beautiful, exploding-with-joy invitation to know Jesus. Read it to deepen your love for Him, and to become more radically aware of God's unending love for you."

—Dominic Done
Author of *When Faith Fails* and Founder of Pursuing Faith (www.pursuingfaith.org)

"For anyone that has ever looked for something better, this book is for you! Through personal and relevant insights, my good friend, Zach Maldonado shows why and how Jesus is better than anything going. This book will lift you up, encourage and inspire you, and reveal just how good God is and how much He loves you. A must read for everyone!"

—Tim Chalas
Lead pastor of Grace Life Fellowship and author of *The Perfect You*

"Reading 'Jesus is Better' is a breath of fresh air for the soul. On every page, Zach invites the reader on a journey of discovering (or rediscovering) why Jesus is truly better, more powerful, more relevant and more vital to your life than you may have ever imagined. Whether you've been following Jesus all your life or you're still kicking the tires trying to figure out whether or not Christianity is true, this book can help you see Jesus in new and remarkable ways."

—Dave Willis
Pastor, podcaster, and author of *Think Like Jesus*

"Zach has provided an invaluable resource, not only for the non-Christian, but the new and seasoned Christian as well. Filled with practical illustrations, undeniable truth, and encouraging stories, *Jesus Is Better* will challenge you to reexamine your relationship with your Savior, while inspiring you to dig deeper into your faith and trust in Him."

—Ryan Weber
Campus pastor at The Journey Church

"Zach Maldonado lays out the truth of the gospel – Jesus is better than anything we use to fix the voids in life. His straightforward approach and examples serve up a scrumptious meal to those who yearn to be fed the truth of who God is and how much the Lord loves His children. I recommend this book wholeheartedly."

—Dr. Scott Hadden
President of Scope Ministries

"Zach has written a great book that will help you rediscover, or maybe discover for the first time, that Jesus loves you more than life itself. It is Jesus who has given His whole self to you for everything you need today. It is Jesus who is better than anything else this world could possibly offer."

—Ross Gilbert
Lead pastor at New Life Fellowship

"Zach is a phenomenal pastor, leader, and friend. Most of all, he loves people no matter their past and wants everyone to see that "Jesus Is Better." This book will cause you to think about your faith, grow in your faith, and share your faith with others. It is definitely a book every person should read."

—Joey Weller
Student Pastor and College Pastor at ChurchUnlimited

"Zach is a front-running next-generation voice for the truths that empower us to actually enjoy the life of Jesus both in and through us. Zach has taken the simple life-giving "Good News" and presented them as they should be i.e. really Good News! Read this book slowly, take notes, highlight passages at will, and write in the margins because you will want to return to these powerful and freeing truths again and again!

—Jimmy Pruitt
Lead Pastor at Bridge Church in Fredericksburg, TX

"Zach uses his own journey and the power of God's word to articulate the truths that people are longing to discover. Every single chapter makes the case for a life of freedom. If you feel weighed down from attempting to live life based on lesser things, I challenge you to take the revelation found in this book and walk out of darkness and into the marvelous light and truth of the reality that JESUS IS BETTER!"

—Larry Goodwin
Lead pastor at The Refuge in Denison, TX

"I wish I had this book in my hands years ago. You will too. Zach Maldonado is a gifted communicator, and he invites you into his story by using relevant illustrations to teach for the first time, or remind you again, that Jesus is indeed better. This book is a must-read, no matter where you find yourself on the journey with Jesus."

—Zac Pruitt
Youth pastor at Graceworks Church

"This book is solid gold! The church desperately needs a resource that is focused on a New Covenant view of Jesus. Zach writes with engaging stories, solid historical evidence, and live changing truth. Sometimes, I find myself trying to measure up in life, but this book is a powerful reminder that JESUS is the end of my search of being enough."

—Cory Hallet
Men's Groups Director at Buckhead Church

"Jesus is Better is an essential read for the "Searcher, Scholar and Skeptic" in all of us. Zach delves into the nature of God in a relatable and easy to understand way that answers the age old question: Is God good? As you are absorbed deeper into the pages, you will find that Yes, God is good and that you will want to recommend this book to all your friends and family."

—Joshua Pinkston
Lead Pastor, Desert Valley Church

"While I might frame a few of the topics Zach Maldonado covers slightly differently, the heartbeat of Jesus is Better inspires me to want to get closer to Jesus' heart. This book reminds us that knowing and following Jesus—and I'm not exaggerating—changes everything. Zach is an excellent guide for discovering a better Jesus: a Jesus who embodies love and invites us all into a life of freedom and abundance. This will be a helpful book for many!"

—Kurt Willems, pastor, spiritual director, and author of
Echoing Hope: How the Humanity of Jesus Redeems our Pain

"I have not read a book like this. It's a perfect mix of new covenant grace and intellectual, systematic, faith defending truth. The church needs more voices like Zach Maldonado. Voices that have the ability to defend the true gospel of Jesus Christ and do it in a way that moves the heart and the mind into a deeper more freeing trust of this new life in Christ. This is a book for everyone. I can't wait to share this book!"

—Caleb Lynch
Lead pastor at Open Door Fellowship Church

THE GOD WHO LIKES AND ENJOYS YOU

JESUS IS
BETTER

ZACH MALDONADO

This book details the author's personal experiences with and opinions about depression. The author is not a healthcare provider. The author and publisher are providing this book and its contents on an "as is" basis and make no representations or warranties of any kind with respect to this book or its contents. The author and publisher disclaim all such representations and warranties, including for example warranties of merchantability and healthcare for a particular purpose. In addition, the author and publisher do not represent or warrant that the information accessible via this book is accurate, complete, or current.

Except as specially stated in this book, neither the author or publisher, nor any authors, contributors, or other representatives will be liable for damages arising out of or in connection with the use of this book. This is a comprehensive limitation of liability that applies to all damages of any kind, including (without limitation) compensatory; direct, indirect or consequential damages; loss of data, income, or profit; loss of or damage to property and claims of third parties.

You understand that this book is not intended as a substitute for consultation with a licensed healthcare practitioner, such as your physician. This book provides content related to physical and/or mental health issues. As such, use of this book implies your acceptance of this disclaimer.

Contents

1 – Is There Another Way? 1

2 – We've Been Tricked 7

PART 1: BETTER THAN UNBELIEF **17**

3 – He's Real 19
Does science point to God?

4 – He's Alive 27
What does history say about Jesus?

5 – He's the Point 37
Can we trust the Bible?

6 – He's the Truth 45
Is there such thing as absolute truth? What's God's will?

PART 2: BETTER THAN RELIGION **55**

7 – He's Different 57
Is there only one way to God? Do we need to fear God?

8 – He's Good 65
Does suffering disprove a good God?

9 – He's Kind 73
How do we reconcile the violence in the Old Testament?

10 – He's Love 83
What sets Jesus apart from religion?

PART 3: BETTER THAN SIN **93**

11 – He Saves 95
What does it mean to be saved?

12 – He Fulfills 105
Is Jesus really enough?

13 – He Teaches 115

How do we hear from God and learn from Him?

14 – He Assures... 125

How does God react when we sin?

PART 4: BETTER THAN SELF-HELP 135

15 – He's Our Comforter 137

Does Jesus care about our day-to-day life?

16 – He's Our Renewer.................................... 145

How does God heal and redeem our hurts?

17 – He's Our Friend...................................... 157

Where is God when we're lonely?

PART 5: BETTER THAN YOUR CIRCUMSTANCES....... 165

18 – He's Our Rest 167

How can we find rest in the midst of terrible circumstances?

19 – He Fights for Us 175

What is God doing in the midst of our depression and anxiety?

20 – He Frees Us... 183

What does it mean that we are free?

21 – He's Our Life 191

What's the abundant life?

Epilogue... 201

Study Guide... 207

Endnotes.. 209

CHAPTER 1

Is There Another Way?

"By his death, Jesus opened a new and life-giving way."
Hebrews 10:20 NLT

Burned out, tired, and weary. This was my experience with Christianity at two different points in my life—during my freshman year of high school and my senior year of college. In both cases I needed answers, hope, and a better way forward.

Go to church camp or on a mission's trip. Get excited. Rededicate. Fail. Try again. Feel guilty for not going to church. Christianity was all about rules for me. I was told to be "more committed" and to "sell out" and "be better" and "be radical." But it never lasted. I'd be nicer to my parents and siblings for the first week after church camp, but then I'd go back to my same old ways. I'd rededicate myself during a Sunday service and would curb my behavior, but it never lasted.

The message was all about modifying my behavior. *Do this. Don't do that. God will love me if ...* seemed to be the mantra for me. I did everything I could think of to make it work. I was always trying to "work on my relationship with God" and "get back right with Him," but it felt like the harder I tried, the worse things got. God wasn't responding, and nothing I did worked.

I memorized Scripture, was a youth leader, and took all the recommended steps. I tried hard, I strived to be better, I read my Bible, and I was dedicated. But nothing made me feel more intimate with God. Nothing fulfilled me. It was all guilt and shame driven. It was legalism, and legalism will never produce contentment, joy, and peace.

I was constantly hearing that God was "searching for true worshipers" or "true Christians," and I always felt like I wasn't qualified to be His or wasn't doing enough to be noticed by Him. I thought God was distant. That He didn't care about my day-to-day life. And that He was angry with me.

I approached my faith in the same way I approached sports. Work harder than anyone else, push through, and eventually I'd see results. But nothing seemed to work. No amount of self-effort or determination made me more obedient or made me feel content.

During my freshman year of high school, I realized I was tired of the legalism I had bought into. I wanted something different. The version of Christianity I was under implied that God was angry at me all the time and wanted me to only serve Him and work for Him. I could never fulfill all the conditional ifs. And even when I did serve Him, it was never enough. At least, that's what I was told by others.

There was always more to do—lots of dos and don'ts—and nothing about my relationship with God changed how I lived life. Sure, I'd give God honor when I scored a touchdown, but the version of Christianity I was believing in offered me no solution or hope for my everyday struggles. It eventually led me to give up and just live for myself.

I spent most of high school living a double life. On the outside, I seemed to be okay, but I was secretly miserable as I pursued fulfillment and happiness in partying, relationships, and sports. It wasn't until my senior year of high school, when I finally got tired of living "like the world," that I decided to give God one more chance.

And He came through. I discovered, in part, His love and grace in new and fresh ways and, after preaching a message at my senior baccalaureate, I knew I wanted to go into ministry. It was my passion!

Fast-forward a few years to my last year of college. I was a youth pastor and felt like my faith was hanging on by a thread. I loved Jesus but didn't know why I wasn't experiencing the rest and abundant life He promised. I wanted to "be enough," and not only did I feel inadequate but I also felt like God wasn't enough for me.

I've noticed that what happens to many of us is that we start out on fire for Jesus, but eventually His love and grace seem to take a backseat. Or we start going through the motions, and the Christian life becomes a chore.

We start out trusting in Jesus's love for us and then, without realizing it, we start striving to earn His love. We begin our journey as Christians, understanding that God is pleased with us because of Jesus, but then, next thing we know, we're trying hard to keep Him pleased. And if you're like me, you spend your time trying to pay God back for all He did for you. "All to Him we owe," right?

Then doubts creep in. Am I really saved or forgiven? Is this bad circumstance coming from God to teach me a lesson? Am I doing enough? All of those questions surfaced as I was trying to teach a bunch of teenagers that God was enough for them. Between my personal struggles and the questions my students kept asking me, I didn't know what to do. I felt like a fraud. Uncertainty about God's existence … my own anxiety … a search for meaning and purpose—all of these things led me to wonder, *Why am I alive? And if God is real, why do I feel so alone and exhausted from life?*

Maybe you can relate. Whether you're just starting college, raising a family, building a career, or now retired, we all come to a point in our life when we are no longer satisfied by our Sunday school faith. We long for something more, something sure, something *better.*

I was struggling with my faith, and what I discovered about God not only changed how I viewed Him and myself, but actually reignited my passion for ministry. The amazing thing is, the message has been there all along. It seemed too good to be true.

The questions my students were asking were the questions I had been asking my whole life. Does science disprove God? Was Jesus a historical person? And what about suffering? I needed to confront them and get real answers. This book is my journey into the freedom, rest, and hope God has promised for you and me. Really, I'm still on the journey. I haven't "arrived." I'm on this adventure. But the answers I've discovered not only changed my life but also made me want to dedicate my entire life to telling people about Jesus.

Your relationship with Christ will be filled with doubt, uncertainty, and struggles, but that's not a newsflash—every relationship is. Doubt isn't something we have to be scared of. Jesus welcomes our doubts. He welcomes our struggles. He invites us to question. As my friend Dominic Done says, our doubt isn't the enemy of our faith; instead, we can embrace our doubt as an opportunity to trust Christ more.[1]

I have struggled with many things and still do. So did the people closest to Jesus. The four Gospels are all about twelve men who constantly doubted Jesus and believed the wrong things about Him. And Jesus never shamed them or condemned them. Instead, He stayed and pointed them to truth. So we're in good company.

Jesus welcomes your failures, your past, your shame, and your regret. I lived for years in shame because of the constant mistakes of my youth. I always thought I was impure, damaged goods, worthless, and not enough. I carried this identity around for years, and my experience in ministry leads me to believe that many of you are believing lies about who you are, and you may not even realize it. This book is a new direction for you, and will not only provide answers to your questions but also offer hope, rest, and freedom in the midst of your struggles and life.

Recently, a friend of mine shared my books and messages with a young woman. Afterward, my friend said, "This young lady grew up in an extremely dysfunctional family. She was sexually abused by her father and sister as a child. The hurt, pain, shame, and self-imposed guilt had crippled her spiritually and emotionally to the point that she felt unworthy to love or be loved by others. She said that, after hearing your message, she felt like it was just for and to her. She said that for the first time in years, she can breathe again."

I have written this book because I want you to enjoy the freedom and life-changing relationship Jesus has for you. It's real. If the version of faith you're experiencing isn't better or more excellent, then it isn't biblical Christianity and it isn't Jesus. He is better, and our relationship with Him is better than anything religion or legalism has to offer (Hebrews 8:6). He promises fulfillment, rest, and freedom, and He is the end to our search of being enough.

There is a "new and life-giving way," as Hebrews 10:20 says. It's a relationship with Jesus that isn't based on what you do or don't do for Him. There are no charts tracking your growth, Bible-reading time, or church attendance. There's no file drawer of your sins or daily checklists. This new and life-giving way is relationship with Jesus. That's it. No strings attached. No hoops to jump through. No membership fees. Just Christ in you.

Religious jargon, Christian clichés, and double-talk have robbed us for too long. This is your invitation to discover the good news of Jesus Christ in a new and fresh way. If you feel like your version of Christianity has worked for others but not for you, then this is the book for you. Your struggles and doubts and questions are welcomed with open arms. You're not less-than for any of the doubts or uncertainties you have. I have them too. We all do.

Whether you have felt misunderstood or have just been searching, I hope this conversation helps spark a fresh awe of Jesus inside you. And I pray you discover the freedom, purpose, and fulfillment that come from truly knowing Jesus.

CHAPTER 2

We've Been Tricked

*"For this reason we must pay much closer attention to what
we have heard, so that we do not drift away from it."*

Hebrews 2:1

When I was in high school, I got tricked. One summer, after a day of work, I pulled into a gas station to fill up my pickup. I went inside to pay for the gas, and when I walked out, a normal-looking guy asked me if I was interested in a brand-new surround sound system. I was seventeen, so of course I was.

I walked over to his truck, and in the back was the brand-new surround sound system he promised me. Nicely packaged in the box. It was a Bose, so I knew it was top-notch. He talked it up and mentioned that he had gotten it as a gift and didn't need it because he already had one similar to it. The box sold itself. The thing looked awesome! And the best part was that it was mine for only $200. That was a deal considering the box had a price tag of $700 on it!

I ran inside, went to the ATM, and got the $200 he wanted, then bought this steal of a deal. I was so excited about my purchase and was pumped to tell my parents the good news! Finally, we would actually be able to hear what we were watching. I opened the box and everything was there—all the speakers and cords and everything. I hooked it up and started trying to test it, and soon realized... I bought a broken sound system. I should have known this deal was too good to be true.

This system was not what I thought, or had been told, it was.

Likewise, growing up, I was sold a counterfeit message about Jesus. I was told one thing and then opened the box of religion and discovered it wasn't what I thought it was. It always seemed that God was mad at me, never pleased, and needy. Many times, I talk to people who describe Him in this way, and I usually say I don't believe in that god either.

Maybe you were never tricked into buying a broken sound system, but for you, you thought Christianity was different from religion, only to later find out there was really no difference in your experience. More money. More serving. More study. More, more, more. Often, the message we hear preached is that we need to do more, be more, and get more. Because we are not doing enough for God and we are not enough.

This double-talk is subtle, and it has caused us to not really believe in the goodness and love of God. Sure, most of us believe we're going to heaven. But we still think God might be out to get us if we don't behave perfectly. By *double-talk*, I mean we're being told two opposing things.

For example, we're told Christ is in us, but then we're told we need to do everything we can to get "closer to God." Or we're told God loves us unconditionally, but then we're told, "He might leave us if we sin too much." We're told God is good, but then we think he causes our suffering. The list goes on and on, and throughout this book we will dispel these common lies and shine a bright light on God's goodness.

Error has creeped into the church and has now become a mainline belief. A recent study found that over 52 percent of Christians think they have to work for God's acceptance.[2] And the same study found that many Christians believe they can do good in order to be saved. This is why many people define Christianity in terms of what they think they can or should do for God. But the good news is all about what Jesus has done for us, not a list of things we need to do for Him.

Most of us start the Christian life with so much energy and joy because we're told that we are free, forgiven, loved, and brand new. But then as we journey on, the good news becomes good advice, and before we know it we become stars of a circus trying to perform for God. That's why Hebrews 2:1 tells us to pay close attention to what we've heard because it's easy to lose sight of the simplicity of the gospel.

Jesus said truth will set us free (John 8:32). So if what we're hearing isn't setting us free, then is it really the truth? This double-talk brings confusion, unrest, and bondage. And yet, Jesus came to give us freedom and rest and peace. And we know He is not a God of confusion (see 1 Corinthians 14:33).

So what if there is a simple and straightforward truth about Him that we can live from? What if Jesus really is good and He really is better than we can imagine?

The Foundation

The version of Christianity that left me so worn out, tired, and broken is a version of Christianity that is still popular today. It's a mix of the Old Covenant and the New Covenant. Many believers think that Jesus is Judaism 2.0. That Christianity is defined by the Ten Commandments and

Jesus. That we need to follow the rules, and if we can't, there's grace. This is why many of us relate to Jesus as if the cross and resurrection changed nothing. We look back to Old Testament characters and think they had it better than us, without realizing that we have something better, something different, and something new.

The problem is that many of us believe our relationship with Christ is centered on what we do for Him. This is Old Covenant thinking. If we think that God's love or our status with Him is based on what we do for Him, then it's no wonder we can never fully enjoy God.

In the Bible, a covenant (or agreement or testament) is between two parties. The Old Covenant was between God and the nation of Israel. Under the Old Covenant, if the people obeyed, God would bless them. If they disobeyed, God would not and there would be consequences. The relationship the people had with God was rooted in their obedience to Him. The problem with the Old Covenant is that people could not "continue" in the covenant (Hebrews 8:9). Why? Humans are faithless and all over the place. The Old Testament is all about Israel's failure to do what God commanded.

So Jesus came and shed His blood for a new covenant and has become the "mediator of a *better* covenant, which has been enacted on *better* promises" (Hebrews 8:6). Not only that, but He "has become the guarantee of a better covenant" (Hebrews 7:22). And as Hebrews 8:13 says, "When He said, 'A New Covenant,' He has made the first obsolete." The New Covenant is not an addition to the Old. It's brand new, different, and better! So what is our job in the New Covenant?

We don't have one. That is the genius of the New Covenant. God took us out of the equation. Hebrews 6:18 says we take refuge and find our hope in "two unchangeable things," which are God and God. God swore by Himself (Hebrews 6:13). This means the covenant is held up by God on one side and God on the other. Our role is simply to accept the free offer of salvation.

This is similar to the covenant God made with Abraham. God put Abraham to rest and He walked alone between the sacrifice. God did this so that the covenant would be upheld by Him alone.

The promises of the New Covenant will never be broken because God cannot lie and God cannot break a promise. So by faith, we simply receive all that God has already done. This is good news because in the Old Covenant, our relationship with God was all about us and our obedience and faithfulness to God. But in the New Covenant, our relationship is all about Jesus and His faithfulness to us.

This changes everything in how we relate to Jesus! Our relationship with Him is rooted in what He has done for us, not in what we do for Him. I spent my entire life thinking God's love for me was based on my love for Him. I thought God blessed me and was pleased with me only if I worked for Him. I thought it was up to me to get right and stay right with God. But the truth is so much better. God's love and delight and blessing for me and you is based solely on Jesus and what He's done. Our relationship with God is not based on us and what we do for Him, but on Jesus and what He's done for us (Romans 5:1).

In the Old Testament, the relationship was transactional. If I do this for God, then God will do this for me. And if you're like me, you've viewed your relationship with God the exact same way. But the New Covenant means we're no longer living for God to do something for us; we're living in response to what Christ has already done for us. We're living *from* Jesus's love, acceptance, and delight in us, not *for* it.

The New Covenant is not the Old Covenant with Jesus added on. It's new and better. Hebrews 7:19 describes the New Covenant by saying we have "a better hope, through which we come near to God." In contrast, the people of God in the Old Covenant could "not approach" Him (Exodus 24:2).

So, what are the foundational promises of the new covenant? Hebrews 8 tells us that we will be God's people and He will be our God (v. 10), no matter what; that we have been given His desires on our hearts and minds (v. 10); and that He remembers our sins no more (v. 12).

Yes, the entire Bible is the inspired Word of God. But not everything written in the Old Testament was for you or is describing you. Indeed, we can learn and grow from what the Old Testament reveals and teaches. But our relationship with God is much better than that of any person who lived under the Old Covenant. This means God is not relating to us on a sin or performance basis. He's relating to us with the same love and affection He has for Jesus (1 John 4:17–18).

Furthermore, Jeremiah, Ezekiel, Moses, and the entire Old Testament longed for the day when the New Covenant would begin. To try to live in both covenants is setting ourselves up for failure. One of the main differences between the Old and the New Covenant is that under the New Covenant, we no longer have deceitful, wicked hearts (see Jeremiah 17:9) like those under the Old Covenant had. But as Ezekiel, Moses, and Jeremiah predicted, we have new, obedient hearts that are naturally pleasing to God (see Ezekiel 36:26; Deuteronomy 30:6; Jeremiah 31:33; Romans 6:17).

Under the New Covenant, we have a forgiveness that is once for all, not year after year. It's based on Jesus's one sacrifice, not the repeated sacrifices of bulls and goats. Under the New Covenant, we are the temple and dwelling place of God. We don't have to go to a place to worship Him. And as we will see throughout this book, the New Covenant changes our identity, the way we relate to God, and even how we live our lives.

In the New Covenant, God treats us like Jesus. He doesn't treat us based on our sin or our performance. The New Testament calls this grace. In a documentary about a famous country singer, he tells the story of playing at a sold-out arena. Tens of thousands of people were there, and as he left the stage, the crowd was chanting his name wanting him to do an encore.

Behind the stage, he saw a concession-stand worker crying. As the crowd was roaring, he asked, "What's wrong?" She responded, "What's it like to be you?" He grabbed her hand and said, "Let's find out." Pulling her on stage with him, he told the crowd, "Treat her like she's me." The crowd went wild and began chanting her name.

This is God's grace. He gives us what we don't deserve or can't earn. He treats us like Jesus forever because Jesus was treated with what we deserved. The stunning announcement of the gospel is that we no longer need to feel the pressure to succeed or be perfect. In Christ, we are accepted, flawless, and valued—even when we fail or don't succeed. This is the remedy for those of us who feel "a pressure to be successful and perfect."[3]

These days I don't buy stuff from people in trucks at convenience stores. I don't want to be tricked into buying something fake. I fact-check everything because I don't want to be scammed again. I used to think God was a fraud, but now I know that I bought a counterfeit and the real thing is better than anything I could ever imagine.

People can give thousands of reasons why they hate God, but what I've noticed is they're usually describing the counterfeit version. In the chapters to come, I hope to show you the God of love and grace who is more about relationship than religion—and who doesn't want you to do more or be better, but just to trust in His love, care, and finished work for you.

Better Than I Imagined

I recently got married, so you will hear a lot about my wife, Grace, in this book. Grace and I had been friends for a while before I summoned the courage to take the next step. I asked her dad to lunch so I could talk to him about my intentions of dating her. (I know, I'm quite the romantic.) He was thirty minutes late, and I felt like I was going to throw up! After I received permission to date his daughter, my next hurdle was to actually convince her to give me a shot.

Long story short, Grace said no. Don't get me wrong, she liked me, but I didn't realize someone had beat me to the punch. It devastated me. I think I spent the whole next week listening to sad country love songs. I followed all the necessary steps to pursue Grace, and I was still rejected.

This kind of thing happens to all of us, especially Christians. We do everything we're supposed to and we're left with nothing. If we're not careful, Christianity turns into a self-help program with the promise that if we obey perfectly, everything in our life will be okay.

This book isn't a self-help manual that promises perfect circumstances. Instead, it's a journey of unlearning things so that we can discover the beauty and truth of Jesus in a fresh way. I absolutely believe, because it's happened to me, that if we embrace the love and grace of Jesus, our lives will be overflowing with freedom, joy, meaning, and peace, because relationship with Jesus always produces those things.

When Grace and I look back, we see it was Jesus who brought us together. I know, that sounds as cheesy as a Hallmark movie. But it kind of is. Four months after she said no, we started talking again, and as they say, the rest is history.

That story is a lot like my journey with Christ. Maybe yours too. At first, y'all were great friends and then you did all the steps to "go deeper" or become "radical," and you were left exhausted and unfulfilled. This was definitely my experience.

In my story and yours too, Jesus never stopped pursuing me, and He will never stop pursuing you. He's in you. And His promise is to never forsake you, even if you lose interest in Him. God isn't wanting you to go deeper or to get radical; He's wanting you to discover His heart for you.

Just like with the rejection I experienced with Grace, Jesus can use the bad experiences you've had with the church and bad theology and turn it into something beautiful and better. He did that with me—not just with Grace, but with my misunderstanding of Him.

Jesus is so much better than I ever imagined. And it was right there in front of me the entire time. I just had to let Him show me. I had to let go of all of the legalism and shame of my past and let Jesus teach me why He truly is *better*. And I had to start looking at everything I had been taught through the lens of the New Covenant. When I did, it changed everything!

PART 1:

BETTER THAN UNBELIEF

"The fool has said in his heart, 'There is no God.'"

Psalm 14:1

"There is the introduction of a better hope, through which we come near to God."

Hebrews 7:19

CHAPTER 3

He's Real

"I do believe; help my unbelief!"

Mark 9:24

I don't remember when I started thinking about God, but I do remember the first time I realized I needed him. When I was nine, my parents told my brother and me they were getting a divorce. I remember crying in bed that night, begging God to intervene. My parents didn't divorce. And I was thankful.

For most of my young life, I treated God like a genie. Even into my adult years, God seemed far off and unconcerned with my everyday life. Eventually, enough pain and bad circumstances led me to start questioning if He was even real.

A recent study done by the Barna Group revealed that "almost half [of Americans] (49%) are not fully confident that God truly exists."[4] I get it. I've always wrestled with God's existence. Is Jesus a myth, fairy tale, or crutch for those who aren't as smart or reasonable as others? And hasn't science proven God doesn't exist? When I was a youth pastor, those were the questions I was asking and my students were asking. It didn't help that

I was taught to believe that faith is blind and that science and faith are not compatible.

Although I used to think God was a myth, a fairy tale, for "dumb people," or something science had disproven, I now believe there's more evidence proving God's existence than there is disproving it. I'm also convinced it takes more faith to *not* believe in God than it does to believe in Him.

Often, we believe something somebody told us without really considering the truth for ourselves. Doubt is normal. I still doubt to this day. But just because we have questions that cause skepticism, doesn't mean our doubt is true. When I discovered the overwhelming evidence for God's existence, it gave me a foundation that I could always lean on in the midst of my uncertainty.

Einstein Was Irritated

Einstein was "irritated" when he discovered that general relativity, his theory, proved the universe had a beginning.[5] General relativity basically states that there has to be a beginning to the universe. Einstein's theory was validated by Edwin Hubble when Hubble, looking through his telescope, revealed that the universe is expanding from a single point in the past.

That means there's an origin to the universe. There's a single point where it all started. Scientists before Einstein believed the universe was simply eternal. But now, virtually every scientist agrees that the universe had a starting point.

This is a game changer. It means something or someone must have created the universe, because something cannot be created from nothing. It needs a cause.

The second law of thermodynamics confirms the universe had a beginning because it states that the universe is running out of energy. For example, I used to always forget to turn off my Game Boy. It ran on batteries, and if I left it on, it would eventually die. One night I was playing it before bed and left it on all night. In the morning, it was dead. Why? Because the batteries had used up their energy.

The universe is like a Game Boy that is dying. It has only so much usable energy left until it dies. Since the universe still has some battery life left, it can't be eternal (the universe isn't dead yet). It must have had a beginning, for if it were eternal, the battery (usable energy) would have already died.[6] This is why virtually every scientist believes the universe had a beginning.[7]

But science can only get us so far. Many scientists explain the creation of the universe by the big bang theory. And it doesn't really explain how the universe was created; it's simply a scientific label saying the universe had a beginning. Even the big bang, when first revealed to the scientific community, was rejected because it seemed to point to the idea that a supernatural being created everything. I definitely think when God said, "Let there be light," there was probably a "big bang" at the beginning. But the question is this: Is there a who—and if not, what caused the universe to exist?

Back to Edwin Hubble for a moment. His telescope's discovery not only confirms the universe had a starting point but also provides evidence that God was the One who created the universe. Here's how: If the universe had a starting point in history, then obviously it began to exist (meaning it's not eternal). If it began to exist, then it must have had a *cause* for its existence. Things don't just begin to exist without a cause. Put simply, nothing cannot create something.

Science itself operates on the principle that all events need a cause. This is called the law of causality. Without the law of causality, science is really impossible. Scientists essentially do one thing—they attempt to discover what caused what. So, based on the law of causality, the second law of thermodynamics, and general relativity, you either believe that God created the universe or, as some atheists do, you ignore those laws and say the universe was created out of nothing.

Since the universe cannot cause itself, the logical conclusion is that the cause is beyond our space-time universe. The cause of the universe must be powerful, uncaused, spaceless, timeless, and immaterial. Which is the Bible's definition of God.

Some of the top scientific atheists and philosophers in the world, when asked about the origin of the universe, say it happened by "magic" or "luck," or use theories based on "imaginary time."[8] Stephen Hawking attempted to explain the beginning of the universe with the theory of imaginary time, but later admitted that his theory is "just a [metaphysical] proposal" that cannot explain what happened in real time. "In real time," he conceded, "the universe has a beginning."[9]

So, which is more reasonable—belief in a creator God or belief in magic, luck, or imaginary time?

This is why Dr. Frank Turek thinks it takes more faith to be an atheist than it does to be a Christian (and I agree). Science *cannot* prove that God doesn't exist. It's an act of faith to be confident that God doesn't exist. One option to not believing in God is to choose to believe in magic, luck, or imaginary time, which takes more faith than believing in what science and reason point to—a Creator. Ultimately, to not believe in God is to reject science and reason.

Then why aren't all scientists believers? It's not because of the facts; it's because of the will. Everyone believes in something, and when that belief is challenged—even by science and facts—we will do everything we can to disprove or talk our way around it. There are plenty of smart people who can articulate a belief, but it doesn't mean they're right.

There's plenty of evidence and science revealing that the earth is round, but you'd be surprised at how many people believe the earth is flat. Even more terrifying is that there are people who deny that the Holocaust happened.

So what if God—an uncaused, eternal, timeless, spaceless, immaterial, personal Being—created the universe? Since God is all of these things, the law of causality does not apply to Him. As Frank Turek says, "The Law of Causality does not say that everything needs a cause. It says that everything that comes to be needs a cause. God did not come to be. No one made God. He is unmade. As an eternal being, God did not have a beginning, so he didn't need a cause."[10]

Put simply, everything that is created has a cause, but since God is not a created being, He doesn't need a cause.

What's more, there's a second piece of evidence that gives even greater clarity and evidence for the existence of God.

Coincidence or Fine Tuning?

Try throwing all the parts of an iPhone down a hill and see if they form exactly the way you want them to on only one try. Odds are, they won't. When you come upon an iPhone or any phone, it is reasonable to think that somebody made it with the intention of making a phone. It didn't just happen by luck or magic. It actually takes over four hundred specific steps to assemble an iPhone.[11]

In the same way, when we look at the universe, with all of its fine-tuned properties that "happened" to perfectly align for the creation of life, it's reasonable to assume that some Being (God) created the universe for the purpose of fostering life.

Chance or designer. Those are really our only two options. When I would come home from elementary school, and my bed was made, clothes were folded, and a snack and juice were on the table ready for me, the reasonable conclusion was my mother did all that. I knew that those things didn't just happen by chance. When we look at how finely tuned our planet is for life, we can either believe it happened by chance or that there was an intelligent designer behind it all.

There are over 122 fine details or constants that make life on Earth possible and provide some of the strongest arguments for God's existence. Geisler and Turek, the authors of *I Don't Have Enough Faith to Be an Atheist*, list some of these as examples[12]:

- Oxygen comprises 21 percent of the earth's atmosphere. That precise figure is an anthropic constant that makes life on Earth possible. If oxygen were 25 percent, fires would erupt spontaneously; if it were 15 percent, human beings would suffocate.

- If the CO_2 level were higher than it is now, we'd all burn up. If the level were lower than it is now, we'd all suffocate.

- If gravity on Earth was altered by 0.00000000000000000000000 000000000000001 percent, our sun would not exist, and neither would we.

- If the earth were any farther away from the sun, we would all freeze. Any closer and we would burn up. Even a fractional variance in the earth's position to the sun would make life on Earth impossible.

All of these constants, if altered slightly, would make life on Earth impossible. Scientist Francis Collins illustrates the inconceivable precision of these constants by saying, "Let's say you were way out in space and were going to throw a dart at random toward the Earth. It would be like successfully hitting a bull's eye that's one trillionth of a trillionth of an inch in diameter. That's less than the size of one solitary atom."[13]

Is this merely a coincidence, or does this point to some common sense—there was a divine designer behind all of what we know as the earth and universe? This is why scientists of all kinds say there is zero chance that another planet could have the same life-giving conditions we have unless there was an intelligent designer behind it.[14]

I haven't even scratched the surface on the evidence for God's existence. There are books upon books from leadings scientists and philosophers who believe in God about how the eye, math, and your mind point to the existence of God. This is why some of the leading thinkers of history and of today believe in God. If we were to put God on trial, the evidence would be clear: He's real.

For example, did you know that your DNA is like a code or a long word that contains over 3 billion characters? Your DNA is a message that has information in it that makes you survive. It is ordered specifically in order to serve a purpose. Do you think that merely happened by accident? That would be like ten thousand books coming into existence because of an explosion at a printing shop. A message requires a messenger. And our DNA points to a designer—God.

Faith is obviously still important for believers, but faith is not blind or dumb. It still takes faith to believe in God, but our faith is not rooted in a fairy tale, but evidence. It's perfectly normal to be faithless. God predicted you would be at times. But He promises that even when you are faithless, He remains faithful (2 Timothy 2:13). God is faithful to constantly point you to truth.

I struggle with insecurity. And one of the things I doubt is whether or not my wife really loves me or if she just settled with me. Sometimes I even wonder if she wants to be married to me. It's not because of something she does. Grace is amazing at constantly reminding me and showing me her relentless love and care for me. But one thing that helps me when I get those thoughts is the wedding ring on my finger. It reminds me of the promise she made to me. The scientific truth of God's existence is a lot like my wedding ring.

That is faith. Walking by faith means walking by facts, not feelings. It means we set our minds on the truth and the evidence about God and what He says about us, not on what we feel moment to moment.

I hope this chapter, and the pages ahead, can act like a wedding ring for you, constantly pointing you back to the evidence when you are doubting and wrestling. The next chapter will not only help your doubt but also give you a rock-solid foundation to rest your faith on.

Since God is real, who is He? The most significant and well-known person in history, Jesus of Nazareth, not only claimed to be God, but also pulled off something that has changed human history forever.

CHAPTER 4

He's Alive

*"Do not be afraid; I am the first and the last, and the living
One; and I was dead, and behold, I am alive forevermore,
and I have the keys of death and of Hades."*
Revelation 1:17–18

When I was in elementary school, I prided myself on how well I could spell words. I always scored the highest on our spelling tests. I have a twin sister, and I always rubbed in how much smarter I was (sorry, Kati). I wish someone had told me that pride comes before the fall.

In our first ever spelling bee, I was confident I would win. I figured I'd be in the newspaper, make the news, and—who knows—maybe even meet the president. When it came to my turn, I proudly stood up, and my teacher said, "Zach, spell *laser.*"

Are you kidding me? I thought. I'd been to laser tag so much that this was the easiest word in the world. With unshakeable confidence, I said, "L-A-Z-E-R. *Lazer.*"

"Not quite," my teacher said.

I had never felt so much embarrassment and shame in my life. The only time I had seen the word laser spelled was at the *lazer* tag place or at the *lazer* car wash down the road. I would have bet my entire life that *laser* was spelled with a *z*.

It's amazing how one small letter or detail can make you completely wrong. I didn't know *laser* was spelled with an *s* because I had never seen it spelled that way or been taught it. It wasn't necessarily my fault; I just didn't know.

Since then, there have been countless examples in my life when I assumed something was true, only to later find out I was wrong. I used to think believing in Jesus was like believing in Santa Claus. But when I did the research, I learned there's more evidence for Jesus and His resurrection than against it.

A lot of us are just as certain about the lies we have believed about Jesus, as I was about the word *laser*. That's why I wrote this book: to help you see the letter we often miss. The letter that I missed for so many years. Even though it was only one letter, it made a huge difference. Often, we can get a lot right about God, but if we get one thing wrong, it makes a huge difference in how we see Him and ourselves.

It seems that every other month, a well-known figure steps away from Christianity. Every single person I've heard about does so for something that really isn't essential to Christianity. The most essential aspect of Christianity is the resurrection of Jesus. Belief in the resurrection of Christ is the most rational thing to believe in once we see the evidence. I've yet to see someone leave Christianity because they could disprove the resurrection.

What History Says

Of all the major world religions, only Christianity claims its founder was resurrected from the dead. Only Jesus, the founder, claimed to be God and then proved it through His resurrection. If you want to disprove Christianity, all you have to do is prove the resurrection didn't happen.

The historical facts surrounding the resurrection are overwhelming and often overlooked when presenting the gospel. I didn't hear these things growing up, and most likely you didn't either. Consequently, we were led to believe that Jesus was just a myth, a fairy tale, or some legend like the Loch Ness monster. I used to think that Jesus contradicted the world of science and reason—that you couldn't believe in both. That's simply not the case.

Here's what we know from history: Jesus existed. Virtually no historian or scholar questions this. One of the leading Bible critics, who's not a Christian, confirms this.[15] And there are ten known non-Christian writers who mention Jesus within 150 years of His life.[16] Most ancient historical figures only have two sources.

According to these ten non-biblical sources, here's what we know: Jesus lived an upright life during the time of Caesar. He performed miracles and had a brother named James. He was pronounced to be the Messiah and was crucified under Pontius Pilate on the eve of the Jewish Passover. Both darkness and an earthquake occurred when he died. Following His crucifixion, His disciples believed He rose from the dead. Because of that belief, His disciples were willing to die, and eventually all but one were killed for their faith. As a result, Christianity spread rapidly as far as Rome.[17]

So we know all of that apart from what the Bible says about Jesus. It's pretty remarkable to me that so much historical evidence about Jesus exists. We also know without a shadow of a doubt that Jesus died. This is a historical fact that no scholar disputes. The Romans were experts at crucifixion, and Roman soldiers were threatened with death to ensure the criminal died on the cross. No record exists of anyone surviving a Roman crucifixion. The certainty of Jesus's death has also been confirmed in an article by the *Journal of the American Medical Association*.[18]

After Jesus's death He was buried in a tomb owned by Joseph of Arimathea, a leader of the Jewish people. It was a well-known tomb, so everyone knew the exact location. Shortly after the resurrection, a rumor was started (and it exists to this day) that His disciples stole the body. That provides further evidence that the tomb was empty. Not only that, but there were also guards, a stone, and a seal on the tomb.

As well, over five hundred eyewitnesses saw Jesus after His resurrection. We know that James, the brother of Jesus, was changed from a skeptic to a believer because of the resurrection. We also know that the apostle Paul was zealous about killing Christians and was changed because of his encounter with the risen Christ. Finally, before the resurrection, nearly all of Jesus's followers had abandoned Him. But after the resurrection? All the disciples except John were killed for their faith in the resurrected Christ. Not one piece of evidence suggests that any of them recanted, meaning they all died believing that Jesus died and rose again.

The only explanation for the rise of Christianity in the first century is the resurrection of Christ. If Jesus had stayed dead, Christianity would be worthless. It all hinged on the resurrection.

Now, consider this. The Watergate scandal in the 1970s was a robbery that tried to cover up illegal activity by Richard Nixon, the president of the United States at the time. The five men involved in the theft were caught, and within two weeks, all five of them, as well as many others, testified against the president. They all recanted. They couldn't keep a lie. Not even for *two* weeks.

Compare that to the apostles who believed in Jesus because of His resurrection. The apostles were stoned, beaten, and eventually killed, and they never recanted. They believed the truth about the resurrection until they died. They never denied Christ or His resurrection. Twelve people don't give their lives for a lie.

Some people question the validity of a miracle like the resurrection since it seems to contradict the laws of nature. But when science cannot explain something, such as the beginning of the universe, the existence of dinosaurs, or some historical event, it looks to the evidence. In the scientific world this is called "inference to the best explanation." The miracle of the resurrection doesn't violate the laws of nature because it was God who supernaturally acted. If God really is the Designer of this universe, then God can intervene when He chooses. Professor of Mathematics at Oxford University, John Lennox, illustrates it this way:

> To argue that the laws of nature make it impossible for us to believe in the existence of God and the likelihood of his intervention in the universe is plainly false. It would be like claiming that an understanding of the laws of the jet engine would make it impossible to believe that the designer of such an engine could, or would, intervene and remove the fan. Of course, he could intervene. Moreover, his intervention would not destroy those laws. The very same laws that explained why the engine worked with the fan in place would now explain why it does not work with the fan removed.[19]

Furthermore, science cannot account for everything, and science and God are not in conflict. Professor Lennox gives another illustration that goes something like this: If you stumble on a pot of boiling water in my house, you can give a scientific explanation for why it is boiling, but you can also give another explanation: I am making tea! These two explanations are not contradicting each other. Instead, they complement each other and actually give a fuller explanation about what is happening.

We simply cannot explain the sudden rise of Christianity except by pointing to the empty tomb. All the evidence is pointing to one thing: Jesus is alive.

My Brother Christian

Christian was born on March 17, 2011. The doctors told us around six months into my mom's pregnancy that Christian had skeletal dysplasia (dwarfism), a hole in his heart, learning disabilities, and a whole host of other issues. When Christian was born two months premature, the doctors were blown away to discover the healthy baby they were looking at. He had none of the conditions they had expected. "A miracle," they said.

About a year later, we discovered that Christian had hip dysplasia (this is the medical term for a hip socket that doesn't fully cover the ball portion of the upper thighbone). That explained why he crawled like an army man all the time, dragging one of his legs. To correct this, he would need surgery and then have to wear a huge cast for six months. But right before the doctors did the surgery, they did another x-ray and said his hip "miraculously fused back into place."

The miracle baby did it again. No surgery needed. He started walking a few weeks later.

There are things in life that our minds and science cannot explain. But that doesn't mean they aren't true or real. I used to think faith and science weren't compatible, but now I realize that science leads us to God.

The greatest pioneers of science—Galileo, Kepler, Pascal, Boyle, Newton, Faraday, and Clerk-Maxwell—were all believers in God.[20]

God has done countless things like this in my life. But even if He hadn't, I would still believe. The evidence is just too compelling for me not to. Not only am I a Christian because of the overwhelming, circumstantial, and scientific evidence for Christ, but also because of my personal story.

He's Alive in Me

For me, the greatest evidence of Christ is what He has done in my life. He's completely changed my desires, satisfied my soul, and given me a life of purpose. I used to love doing sinful things, but as I've come to know Jesus more and more, I no longer desire to do the things I used to. I tried to find myself in all the things this world had to offer, and I would always fall asleep each night wondering, *Am I enough? Is this all that life has for me?*

Jesus alone meets that need. Some guy smarter than me once said something along the lines of, "We've all got a God-shaped hole in our heart." And I can attest to that. I tried so hard to fill that hole with things of this world. It wasn't until I filled that hole with Christ that I finally felt like life made sense.

I no longer have to fear death because of the resurrection. I no longer need to wonder what my worth or value is because Jesus showed me that I'm worth enduring the cross to Him. We don't have to wonder where God is. Because we're in Christ, He's in us. Forever. And even though we may not feel the presence of God's love and Spirit in us, we can know that no matter what we feel, we are totally loved and forever indwelt by God Himself.

I believe Christ lives in me. It's not a feeling. But there have been many instances in my life when He's revealed Himself to me. Not only that, I've experienced Him through His people. I've never been more loved and cared for than by other believers. Some Christians can be judgmental and mean. We don't behave perfectly. But behaving perfectly is not our message. Our message is about the One who came to rescue us because we didn't have it all together.

This Jesus, who created the entire universe, gave Himself for us through the cross and the resurrection so that He could forever live in us. He loves you. Yes, you. No matter who you are or what you've done. His love for you is not based on what you do, but on who He is. You cannot exhaust His love. He doesn't get tired of loving you.

Since the tomb is empty, we don't have to be. In Christ, you are complete and whole (Colossians 2:10). You lack nothing (1 Corinthians 1:7; 2 Peter 1:3). Jesus's dying for your sins is only part of what He did; His resurrection to give you new life is the other part.

Most of us have never really considered what it means to be given new life. The resurrection is not only proof that Jesus exists; it's also the very doorway into experiencing Him every moment of every day. I lived most of my life trying to live the Christian life, not realizing that the Christian life is not a life lived by my best effort. The Christian life is lived by trusting the risen Christ inside of us.

My favorite thing about my wedding was seeing my bride walk down the aisle. We were engaged for a year and had been dating for nearly three. So much anticipation culminated on that day. The entire day, I felt so much excitement and nervousness. It was the day I'd been waiting for and praying for my entire life.

Grace had warned me about a long pause between the ringbearers walking down the aisle and her entrance. After what seemed like an eternity, the bridal music started, and it felt like the beat dropped (I think they call that the crescendo). She appeared from the top of the steps and ... whoa! She was perfect. Beautiful. Stunning. As tears flowed from my eyes, there was no doubt in my mind that I loved her and she was the only thing I could focus on. Every fiber of my being was overwhelmed with love, and I was so in awe of my bride. I'm not a crier—at all—but the tears flowed like a raging river!

The Bible says we are the bride of Christ—that we are in union with Jesus, just like a married couple—except as believers we have something even better than human marriage: we are joined spiritually to Christ. We are literally one spirit with Him (1 Corinthians 6:17).

Do you realize what Christ (the Groom) thinks about His bride (you and me)? Masterpiece, set apart, wonderfully made, flawless, adored. Don't let anyone tell you otherwise. The resurrection means that you are perfectly close, totally accepted, unconditionally loved, and forever adored by Jesus. No matter what you've done or what you do, Jesus, your Groom, doesn't regret saving you.

The amount of love and awe and excitement I felt (and still feel) for my bride, Grace, is a drop of water compared to the ocean of love God has for you, His perfect bride. Jesus has never looked at you and wished He saw someone else. Have you taken a look in your Groom's (Jesus's) eyes lately?

CHAPTER 5

He's the Point

You examine the Scriptures because you think that in them you have
eternal life; and it is those very Scriptures that testify about Me; and
yet you are unwilling to come to Me so that you may have life.

John 5:39–40

Discovering that the Easter bunny wasn't real was *devastating* to me. He or she or it was the last character I was holding out on. I grew up with four siblings, so Santa and the tooth fairy were quickly falsified. But for whatever reason, I was older when I discovered the Easter bunny wasn't real—maybe third grade. Each year for Easter, we would always get a basket from the Easter bunny, which was clear evidence of its existence.

At the time, we were going to church in Austin, about a forty-minute drive from our house. I remember wondering why there hadn't been an Easter basket when I woke up. It was in the car in the church parking lot that my parents told me the truth. I may have cried. Don't judge me.

Maybe it wasn't the Easter bunny for you, but you learned something about your faith that shook you. It made you question everything. Many of us think the Bible is like the Easter bunny—just a legend, fable, or myth.

Unlike the Easter bunny, though, when I heard the truth about the Bible, it didn't devastate me; it set me free. We think Jesus is for kids and that once we reach adulthood, we don't need Him anymore. But as we've seen, it's more reasonable and logical to believe in Jesus than not to believe in Him.

A quick trip to Google or Reddit will reveal all sorts of claims from skeptics and atheists about the Bible, Jesus, and God. The world is filled with fake news. The moment we hear an assertion by a college professor or a claim on a YouTube video, we assume it's true. That's why I wrote this book. I wanted to present the evidence and let you be the judge of it. I used to believe the Bible was a made-up story about Jesus, but now I believe the Bible is a divinely inspired compilation of books about God's love for you and me.

It's good to question what we believe. It's good to fact-check what we hear. A good student doesn't just listen to one side of the argument. Time and again, the truth about Jesus found in the Bible has held up to thousands of years of scrutiny. Just on the historical and scientific evidence alone, it's reasonable to believe in Jesus and what He's done. You may be wondering, *But hasn't the Bible been changed or proven false? Isn't the Bible filled with errors or contradictions? Is it really historically reliable, or is it outdated and irrelevant?*

As I said in the last chapter, the resurrection is the basis and foundation of our faith, not the Bible. Now don't get me wrong. I believe the Bible is the inspired Word of God. But our faith rests on the event of the resurrection of Christ, not on merely what the Bible says. See the difference? This actually means that we can disagree on certain things in the Bible and still be friends and you can still be a Christian.

This isn't a full and detailed argument about the reliability of the Bible; that has already been made by many others.[21] However, I want to show you why the four writers who wrote the most about Jesus can be trusted, and then reveal what Jesus said about the rest of the Bible. Ultimately, my goal is to help you realize that we can trust what the Bible says.

You Can Trust the Bible

The New Testament was written as early as fifteen years after the ascension of Jesus. The four Gospels, which primarily tell about the life of Jesus, were written twenty to fifty years after the ascension. The reason this is important to note is because they were written during the lifetimes of those who knew and/or witnessed Jesus. This means the writers couldn't have made up what they said, because they would have been easily discredited by those who actually saw the events take place.

A renowned non-Christian archaeologist, Nelson Glueck, said, "No archeological discovery has ever contradicted a biblical reference."[22] This is why the majority of scholars and historians—both atheist and Christian—conclude that the New Testament, and specifically the Gospels, are the most reliable and credible documents from the ancient past.[23]

For example, Luke wrote the Gospel of Luke and the book of Acts and records thirty-two countries, fifty-four cities, and nine islands without a single mistake.[24] Furthermore, there are over eighty-four confirmed historical and archaeological facts in the book of Acts, which is why most historians say that Luke is one of the best (if not the best) historians in his time.[25]

If Luke and the other Gospel writers were so accurate with their history, then perhaps they were also accurate with what they said about Jesus. So we don't believe in the Bible because some religious person told us to. We can trust in what the Bible says about God because the Bible has proven to be true by the historical and archeological evidence.

Most ancient documents that are considered trustworthy and historical have less than *twelve* manuscript copies and those copies were written 400 to 1,500 years after the original was written. The New Testament has over *5,600* handwritten manuscript copies that were written within just 25 years of the original. Those are just the ones in Greek. There are over 25,000 manuscript copies of portions of the New Testament in existence today written in different languages.[26] The next closest work is *The Iliad* by Homer, with 643 manuscripts.[27]

For example, there are two surviving biographies of Alexander the Great that are viewed as historical and accurate, and they were written 400 years after Alexander died. The New Testament has portions written 25 years after the original. Copies of most of the New Testament exist today that were written just 150 years after the original.

Homer's *Iliad* was copied with a 95 percent accuracy. By comparison, it is estimated the New Testament is about 99.5 percent accurate.[28] Yes, there are variations in the manuscripts. Some have estimated over 200,000 variations. But 75 percent of the variants are spelling differences like *John* may be spelled with one n or with two.[29] Clearly, this doesn't jeopardize the meaning of a text. The others have to do with synonyms and the fact that some manuscripts call Jesus by His proper name or by "Lord" or "He."[30] But there are zero, zilch, nada variants that affect a core Christian belief.

So contrary to the atheist on YouTube, the Bible hasn't changed or been proven false. Instead, history and archaeology and the thousands of copies reveal that we can trust what we read.

Look to Jesus

Tom was sitting in a park playing checkers with a monkey. As they played game after game, a large crowd gathered around to watch them. The people were amazed and talked among each other about the monkey who could play checkers. Tom became really annoyed at the chatter and said, "I don't know why you think he's so great. I have beaten him eight out of ten games!"

Have you ever missed the point? (Or the joke?) This story demonstrates how easily one can miss the point. The Bible says that Jesus had to explain that He was the entire point of the Old Testament. Usually, we get so focused on the commands and sayings that we miss the point. We miss Jesus.

That was my version of Christianity. I thought Jesus loved me but I needed to do ten things in order for Him to keep loving me. I was as committed as they come, but nothing I did made me feel closer to Jesus or more loved by Him. I went to every Bible study, went to every camp, and was even mentored by my youth pastor for a season in order to learn more about the Bible. Talk about extra credit. For whatever reason, I missed it. I thought the Bible was ultimately about me and what I needed to do for Jesus.

I thought grace was for the unbeliever—and that as a believer, I'd better be "more committed" and "serve God more" and "follow the rules." All of that felt like I was a servant in a king's house instead of a son in his Father's house. I knew God's grace saved me, but I still believed it was up to me and my good works to keep me saved and keep God happy.

Then I was introduced to God's grace. Now I can't read the Bible without seeing it all over. I finally realized that the Bible is primarily about Jesus and what He's done for you and me. It's about His pursuit of relationship with the world. It's not about our commitment to God but His commitment to us. It's about how Jesus came to make us friends, not slaves. Through Him we truly are beloved sons, not wicked servants. I believed the message that I "owed God" and my life as a Christian was about me trying to pay him back. But Jesus is not asking you to live your life trying to repay the grace He has lavished on you. He is asking you to live your life enjoying the grace He has lavished you with (Ephesians 1:8).

If Jesus rose from the grave like history and the Bible claim, then we can trust what Jesus says and what Jesus affirms—the Bible. The Bible isn't a bunch of rules Jesus is asking us to keep. The Bible is a collection of sixty-six books written in multiple languages over 1,500 years by about forty different authors. It is inspired by God. How can we know it's inspired by God and trustworthy? The fact that forty different authors, in many different genres over 1,550 years, all pointing harmoniously to Jesus, would be impossible to duplicate.

The Bible reveals to us a narrative of God's love, mercy, and grace for His people. Hundreds of good books have been written on how to interpret the Bible, but one thing we need to know is that it's all about Christ and His plan to rescue and save us.

The Bible is ultimately what God has done for us, not what we need to do for God. Over and over again we see God's rescue in the midst of our rebellion. His radical grace overcoming our guilt. His unending mercy in the midst of our mess. His Son for our sin.

Furthermore, we can look to God's written Word, the Bible, to see who God is, who He's made us, and what He wants from us. As we come to understand that truth, it sets us free. Yes, there are some difficult passages and things that *seem* outdated, but I believe when you interpret them in light of the cross and resurrection and their cultural background, we see good news at the heart of it.

I love when I receive notes and texts from my wife. They make my entire day. One of the ways I receive love is through words of affirmation, and Grace does an amazing job of affirming me and reminding me of who I am and what I mean to her. One of my favorite things to do is go back and re-read those notes. Every time I read them, it's like getting a hug or kiss from Grace. And what's even better than the note? Her telling me in person.

The Bible is similar to that. God has shown us His love and character and His opinion of us in His Word. The Bible doesn't need to be a "discipline" we feel like we need to do. Instead, it's a love letter from the One who loves us the most. We get to read and discover the character of God and His extravagant love for each of us.

I used to think reading the Bible was about pleasing God or doing my Christian duty. I now see that reading the Bible is about getting to know Jesus more. We're not reading about some dead historical teacher. No, Jesus the Teacher, Healer, and Savior is living within us now. And by His Spirit, He teaches and reminds us of all that He has said and done.

Don't get me wrong, it can sometimes be difficult to read Scripture. There's no power in "reading." The power comes from *what* we are reading. It's God's truth that sets us free. You don't have to understand the Bible perfectly to be a Christian. We can actually disagree on a lot in the Bible and still be Christians. To be a Christian means to believe that Jesus is Lord and that God raised Him from the dead. As I said earlier, Christianity is rooted in the resurrection, not whether or not we can pass a Bible quiz.

Jesus isn't Dwayne Johnson, "the Rock." He isn't some celebrity that we simply know about. There's a big difference between knowing about a celebrity and knowing your best friend. Jesus is Someone we get to know personally. He's our Friend. The more I get to know Jesus, the more I realize He simply wants to be with me, be my friend, and love me. No strings attached. That's what makes Christianity different from any other religion: we get to personally know the God who came to live in us.

CHAPTER 6

He's the Truth

Jesus said to him, "I am the way, and the truth, and the life;
no one comes to the Father except through Me."

John 14:6

I struggle with change. I like my days planned out, and I like what is familiar to me. Change is scary because it feels like I lose control. My wife and I use the phrase "get your body ready" on pretty much a daily basis. It's how we start a sentence that involves change. For example, "Hey, babe. Get your body ready. I'm going to lunch with my friend tomorrow." We try to eat lunch together most days, so we try to give each other a heads-up so we can get emotionally ready for a change of plans. I know this sounds crazy, but we like being together. Neither of us likes changing our normal routine.

Harry Truman (no, not the president) lived by a stratovolcano (a fancy word for volcano) in Washington State. In 1980, the volcano was showing signs of erupting, and eventually many experts said it had a 100 percent chance of erupting and that everyone should evacuate. Not only would it erupt, but the path of the volcanic flow would go right through where Harry lived.

Of course, Harry left because his family and the local government told him to leave, right? No. Harry didn't like change either. He didn't want to leave his home. Even if it meant his own death.

We may not live in the shadow of an active volcano, but for many of us change is scary. Often, we resist change because we are uncomfortable with leaving what is familiar to us. This is how truth can feel. No one likes to be proven wrong. It's humbling. So we turn into defense attorneys, resisting and fighting until we finally see the truth. I used to believe truth was based on someone's personal opinion, but I now know that God determines truth. The change was hard, but trusting Jesus is always worth it.

Would you agree that crimes like rape and murder are wrong? How about the Holocaust or the abuse of helpless children? If yes, then would you also agree that this isn't merely your opinion? I don't have to persuade you or anyone to believe those things are wrong. We simply know they are. All reasonable people recognize certain things as evil. This proves something: moral values and standards exist, no matter your beliefs about God. The question then is, how do we know this?

Fifty-eight percent of Americans say that "moral standards are decided by the individual,"[31] and only 42 percent of us believe that God is the basis of truth.[32] This means that, if you're reading this, there's a good chance you agree with the statistics. But if you agreed with the previous paragraph, then you do believe that there are moral standards that exist apart from one's personal opinion. These are called objective or factual moral standards.

If you agree that there are objective moral standards, that supports the argument for the existence of God because every law has a lawgiver. Since there are obviously objective moral laws (like murder and rape), there must be a moral lawgiver—God. If moral standards are decided by the individual, that means you can believe murder and rape are just an opinion. I am sorry, my friend, but if your view of the world requires you to believe that rape and murder are okay, then I think you're wrong.

It's okay to be for something and against something else. It's also normal and okay for people to disagree with you. However, just because you are for something doesn't mean you are against everything else. If you like hamburgers, that doesn't necessarily mean you don't like hot dogs. To say that we believe God is the standard for morality isn't to say that people can't make decisions for themselves. Let's use reason and follow the evidence and logic so we can believe in what's really true.

In a world without God, morality would only be an opinion. It wouldn't be grounded in anything but the shifting attitudes of humans, who are constantly changing. It makes more sense to ground our morality in Someone who is unchanging, just, and good.

Often, people wonder how there can be so much evil if God exists. But those who reject God because of evil have to borrow the biblical concept of good and evil in order to know evil exists. Simply put, the existence of evil is proof since God is the standard of good. God can exist without evil, but evil cannot exist without God. Evil is like rust on metal. You can have metal without rust, but you cannot have rust unless there's metal. Evil is only realized and seen in the context of good. That is why when something evil is done, we call it *im*moral, *un*just, or *dis*honest.

So, evil doesn't disprove the existence of God. It actually points to an objective good that exists in this world, because we all recognize objective evil (murder, rape, etc.). Therefore, there has to be objective good. And if there is objective good, then there's a God.

C. S. Lewis was once an atheist who thought the existence of evil disproved God. But he came to realize, "[As an atheist] my argument against God was that the universe seemed so cruel and unjust. But how had I got this idea of just and unjust? A man does not call a line crooked unless he has some idea of a straight line. What was I comparing this universe with when I called it unjust?"[33]

The Truth About Truth

Haven't you noticed that we demand truth in everything except our faith and our morals? We want doctors to be right when they prescribe us medicine. We want our bankers to make sure they give us the correct amount of money and our financial advisors to be honest. In almost every area of life, we expect truth. But when it comes to morals, we (as a society) don't.

A popular notion about truth is that something is "true for you but not for me." But that argument doesn't work anywhere else in life. Try going to the bank and withdrawing $1 billion out of your account. When the teller says, "Sorry, you only have $123.47," you say, "That's true for you but not true for me. Give me the money." Think that will work? Of course it won't.

I can believe that gravity doesn't exist, and every single time I jump off a ledge I will be met with the reality that gravity is indeed real. Why? Well, my "truth" is merely an opinion if it's not grounded in reason and reality. That is why you cannot have two "truths" that contradict each other.

Truth is not something that is invented. It's something that is true for all people, and it exists apart from anyone's knowledge of it. 4+4=8 for every single person. Gravity existed long before Newton discovered it. That is why it's important for us to understand that a belief is different from truth.

Someone can sincerely believe that 4+4=10, but it doesn't change the truth. It just means they're sincerely wrong.

As much as I resist change, one of the things that I constantly notice about myself is how much I can change my mind or opinion about something. I'm not always certain. That's why I don't want the standard for morality to be based on my opinion, nor do I want truth to be based on what I feel today. I also don't want to live my life based on the opinions Instagram is telling me to believe. If the resurrection is really true, then I am going to base truth and morality on God, not my feelings or opinion.

He's the Truth

Since God is Creator, He knows His creation and what is best for us. The truths He's given us are sufficient, relevant, and trustworthy. His guiding ethic for us is love. And He is love. That's what we look to and lean on. Love is our guide. Love doesn't steal, kill, or hurt someone. And as we see throughout the New Testament, love is the overflow of our relationship with the God who is love.

As Truth, God gives us a foundation to live our lives from. We no longer have to search for acceptance and love from what we do or from what others think about us. God has announced to us that we are accepted and loved apart from what we do or don't do (Romans 15:7; 8:38–39). We no longer have to live based on our emotions; we get to live from God's truth about who we are. We are God's masterpiece (Ephesians 2:10 NLT). Complete, righteous, holy, beloved. Our identity as God's children is based on what He's done, not what we do. It's based on the truth of God's Word, not our feelings.

This is why we can live our entire lives from God's acceptance and love of us, not for it. We can live our lives knowing that we are God's children, completely righteous and blameless. We do not have to work in order to achieve status with God. What He's done through the cross and resurrection has secured our place as His children forever. And the truth about our identity is a firm foundation we can live from.

He's the Way

"Jesus is the Way" means He's not only the way to be saved, but He's also the guide into all fulfillment and satisfaction in our lives. He's the way to meaning and purpose. This is found in understanding God's will. God's will for your life is simple and straightforward. It is not a secret step-by-step plan or a mystery that we have to figure out.

Before we look at what Scripture says is God's will, remember this: you are right with God and forgiven (Romans 5:1; Colossians 2:13). As I've talked with people about God's will for their lives, they usually have a fear that if they don't make the right decision, then God will be mad and they may lose their status with Him. They often think they have to perform or behave perfectly in order to stay in God's will.

But our righteousness and forgiveness do not come from doing everything right. Our righteousness is given to us because Jesus did everything right on our behalf. And our forgiveness is solely based on Jesus and His shed blood. We're righteous because of Jesus's obedience, not ours. Romans 5:19 tells us this: "Through the obedience of the One the many will be made righteous." We're forgiven because of Jesus's finished work and sacrifice, not our constant work or sacrifices (Hebrews 10:17). So our status with God is based on what Jesus did, not on the decisions we make.

This means that God's attitude toward us is not affected by how well we perform or do His will. His presence in us is always there. His love for us is never ending. And His grace will never run dry. God does not bless us based on how we live. Instead, we are blessed with every spiritual blessing the moment we trusted in Christ (Ephesians 1:3).

This also means that we can't make a wrong decision and "miss out on God's best" for us. God's best for your life is not a certain circumstance. The best thing God can do for you is give you Himself, and He does that fully at the moment of salvation.

God's will is His desire. When you think of the word *will*, don't think of a detailed plan but of desire. This is what *will* means. The will of God is His desire for our life. And we can understand and know God's will (see Ephesians 5:17). God's will is not a step-by-step plan that we go in and out of; instead, it is His desire for us in every moment. And His will is clearly taught throughout the New Testament. God's will is that we rejoice, pray, and give thanks:

> "Rejoice always; pray without ceasing; in everything give thanks; for this is God's will for you in Christ Jesus." 1 Thessalonians 5:16–18

We can rejoice in what God has done for us, in what God has done to us, and in what God is doing through us. Further, God wants us to talk to Him. The instruction "pray without ceasing" does not mean every second of every day. It means God desires for us to speak to Him because He loves to hear about everything we are going through and doing. And He desires that we give thanks *in* everything, not *for* everything. He is not asking that we give thanks for our bad circumstances or for the bad things that may happen to us. No, He is saying that we can give thanks in everything because in everything, we have all that we need in Him.

God's will is that we do what is right and pleasing to Him:

"Equip you in every good thing to do His will, working in us that which is pleasing in His sight, through Jesus Christ." Hebrews 13:21

"For such is the will of God that by doing right you may silence the ignorance of foolish men." 1 Peter 2:15

God's desire is that we live out of who He has made us. Why? Because the opposite of this would be to live in sin. God knows what is best for us and wants us to be fulfilled by walking after Him. Here's the cool thing: we can please God by what we do. He delights in us every time we trust Him and express His Son. Not only does He delight in who we are, but He also delights in what we do in dependence on Him.

However, our sin and bad behavior never make us fall out of God's will or plan for our life. God's will isn't some plan that hinges on our every decision; it is His desire for us in every moment. That's why we can choose to do God's will, no matter the circumstance.

We also see throughout the New Testament that God's will is for all people to believe, be saved, be set apart, and come to repentance (see 1 Timothy 2:4; 2 Peter 3:9; 1 Thessalonians 4:3-4; John 6:40). I love God's heart. He wants everyone to be saved. And He is pursuing everyone with His reckless love. He truly loves the world (John 3:16). And He loves you. We can trust in the character of God because His character is love.

God's desire for us is to look to His Son and believe in Him. He wants us to be sanctified in what we do. Sanctified means set apart. And the good news is, God has sanctified you as a person, once and for all (Hebrews 10:10, 14; 1 Corinthians 1:2; 6:11). So God is calling us to align our behavior with our identity—to live sanctified because we are sanctified.

God's desire for us is to not be overwhelmed by our sins or our circumstances. Instead, He wants us to gaze at His Son, the One who has taken away our sins. God's will is that we look to Jesus in every moment, knowing that He is enough.

We are all faced with tough decisions in life. And we all ask the same question: "What is God's will for me in this moment?" In these moments, God wants you to use wisdom, to talk to trusted friends, and to choose freely. Whatever decision you make, God is in you through it. He's in you and with you no matter the decision you make. God gives us a lot of freedom to make decisions in our lives because no matter what we choose, He's with us, and we can carry out His desire whether we take job A or job B.

That is the great thing about God's will. You can do it anywhere. Essentially, God's will can be summed up by being loved and loving others. As we learn to trust Jesus and receive His love in every moment, we will love others. We will talk to Him, we will give thanks, and we will live out who He's made us.

Jesus is better than unbelief because Jesus gives you meaning, purpose, and more than just this temporal life.

PART 2:

BETTER THAN RELIGION

"I hate, I despise your religious festivals; your assemblies are a stench to me."
Amos 5:21 NIV

*"But now He has obtained a more excellent ministry, to
the extent that He is also the mediator of a better covenant,
which has been enacted on better promises."*
Hebrews 8:6

CHAPTER 7

He's Different

"For the Son of Man has come to seek and to save that which was lost."
Luke 19:10

Jesus is the only person who welcomes our failures. I fail—a lot. My life is littered with failure. This is why I'm so thankful the goal of the Christian life is not to "live victoriously" but rather trust in the One who is victorious. Often, our failure drives us to give up, to feel hopeless, to think God has given up on us.

Growing up, when I failed, the last thing I wanted to do was go to my dad. I knew he loved me, but I was convinced that my failures would somehow make him love me less. Religion does this too. When we mess up, we think we're supposed to remember our failures. Religion led me to hide from God when I failed, not go to Him.

Our failures are the reason Jesus came to die for us. He's drawn to people who have failed because people who have failed are the only people there are. Jesus comes to us in our failures not to shame us or condemn us but to save us and comfort us. Jesus is different from any other person or world religion or system because our failures don't disqualify us from His love. They are our ticket into His love. Our failures don't define us; Jesus does. In our failures, God is inviting us to remember His faithfulness and finished work on the cross, not our mistakes.

If you're *not* hearing words like *saint, child,* and *loved* when you sin and mess up, then it's not coming from Jesus. Only God defines us and gives us our name. Our failures don't. And His name for us stays the same. We're His children, no matter what. In every single failure, we never burden God or cause Him to question His devotion to us.

Shame tells us that we are not _____ enough. You fill in that blank. Maybe for you, it's not skinny enough, smart enough, or good enough. Shame lies to us and says that if someone knew who we really were, we wouldn't be loved or accepted. Jesus enters into that and says, "I love and accept you." Jesus has seen everything about you—the good, the bad, the ugly—and loves everything about you. Nothing you do can change His mind about you.

Religion and Jesus are completely different. The difference is like driving on a freeway or a toll road. Many of us think Jesus is like a toll road. That every so often we have to stop and pay a fee. That's religion though. Religion is always trying to get us to do or pay for what's already been done. The way of Jesus is a *free*way. (You see what I did there?) There's no toll booth awaiting us at any point in our relationship with Him.

It's easy to buy the lie that God is irritated or frustrated or even disappointed in us. We tend to believe that we've ruined our usefulness for Him. But Romans 11:29 declares to us that "the gifts and the calling of God are irrevocable." God will never take back His acceptance, His love, or His calling of you. Those promises are yours to keep no matter your performance.

God on Top of the Mountain

I once heard a pastor tell this story: He was sitting outside a Buddhist temple in Indonesia where he was engaged in a conversation with a Buddhist leader and a Muslim leader. They were discussing how all religions are fundamentally the same and only superficially different. The Buddhist and Muslim leader basically believed that all religions agreed on the essential issues.

They asked the Christian pastor what he thought, and he said, "It sounds as though you both picture God at the top of a mountain, and we are all at the bottom of the mountain. One religion may take one path up, and another religion may take another, and in the end, we all end up in the same place, at the top."

They replied, "Yes! You understand!"

Then the Christian pastor said, "What would you think if I told you that the God at the top of the mountain came down to where we are? What would you think if I told you that God doesn't wait for people to find their way to him, but instead He comes to us?"

The Buddhist and Muslim leaders thought for a second and then responded, "That would be awesome."

He replied, "Let me introduce you to Jesus Christ."

I'd like to add to this story. Not only did God come down, but He rescued us and then went back up the mountain and seated us with Him. Ephesians 2:6 says we are seated with Christ in heaven. The Christian life is not about us working our way to God, but trusting that God worked His way to us. Jesus's deepest desire is for you to be with Him (John 17:24). Christ in you means He is now closer to you than He was to His own disciples.

That is the difference between Christianity and other religions. Religion is about what you do for God. But Christianity is about what God has done for you. Religion is about proving your love and worth to God. But Christianity is all about how Jesus proved His love for you and revealed your worth by dying for you.

In religion, you have to meet the requirements in order to be accepted and pleasing to God, but in Christianity, Jesus has met those requirements for us. Religion is all about rules. Jesus is all about relationship. That's the main point. Jesus doesn't need you. He doesn't need you to be His slave, to be His worker. He wants you for one reason—relationship. The Christian life isn't about us trying to keep an angry God pleased; it's about us trusting in a loving God who's already pleased.

Jesus is not our example or our role model. He's our Savior. Christianity is not about following a dead person's teaching. Christianity is about Christ living His life in you and through you as you have relationship with Him. Christianity is not about managing our sin in order to please God. Christianity is about trusting in the one who took away our sin forever. God isn't asking you to earn His love, but to enjoy His love.

Buddha's dying words were "Strive on, untiringly." Jesus's last words were "It is finished." I'll take Jesus. I'll take Jesus because my hope isn't in being good enough, and my hope isn't in accomplishing a bunch of good works. My hope isn't in my strength, my best effort, my faithfulness, my obedience, or my dedication or commitment to God. God isn't asking us to live a "victorious Christian life." He's inviting us to know and trust the victorious Christ.

My hope—our hope—is in Jesus Christ alone.

Only One Way?

In every religion, there's no security—no way of knowing if you're enough and if you'll ever do or be enough. In every major religion, you have to be obedient and live right to be saved. If the resurrection is true, as we've shown, then Jesus is truly the only way to God. Which is actually really good news for us. But is this fair? Why can't there be many ways to God? If Jesus is so loving, then why not accept everyone?

Christianity is both inclusive and exclusive. Inclusive in the fact that anyone can join. Exclusive in the fact that there's only one way to God, through Jesus, and you have to say yes. Perhaps you've been called "narrow-minded" for believing that. But just because we or others don't like something doesn't mean we need to discredit it. Let's examine it and see if it holds up to scrutiny.

"Fair" is an opinion. What is fair? According to our standard or God's? No one is entitled to salvation. And no one deserves to be saved. This is what makes God's grace so unfair: it's a free gift! And I'm putting all of my confidence in the belief that every single person will have an opportunity to say yes or no to Jesus.

If there were many ways to God, how would we know which was right? If it were based on works or right living, how would we know if we ever did enough? Christianity is the only belief system that offers salvation freely by grace. It's not narrow-minded or judgmental to believe this, especially since our message is not a secret. The offer of salvation is not being hidden from people. God wants all people to come to repentance, and we can trust in God's goodness that everyone will have a chance to be saved.

The gate of salvation is narrow because only Jesus saves. What's crazy is that most people would rather earn, work for, or achieve salvation instead of letting Jesus save them. That's the wide road of religion—performance, achieving, and striving. The narrow gate is entered by humility. We simply say, "We can't save ourselves, Jesus, but You can."

So why can I trust in Jesus?

As we saw earlier, there is overwhelming proven evidence about the resurrection and the early church and the Scriptures. Since Jesus is alive, then everything He said must be true. Since the New Testament is reliable, we can trust the claims it makes. Furthermore, not only did Jesus claim to be God, but He pulled it off. He rose from the dead.

Jesus is the way, the truth, and the life, and no one can go to the Father except through Him (John 14:6). We can never be good enough or do enough good works to be saved. Jesus said the standard was perfection. None of us are perfect. But then He became our sin and told us that He has met the standard for us. Jesus is a gentleman, and He will never force anyone to say yes to Him. He's pursuing the entire world, wishing none to perish.

All it takes is trust in Jesus. That's it. Jesus will not force anyone to be saved. He is drawing people to Himself by His love and kindness. He doesn't force people to love Him back. He wants them to freely choose. And He's inviting everyone to a life-giving relationship that is more than going to heaven one day. It includes His love, care, and friendship with us right now. We get to come to Jesus, mess and all. He isn't asking us to clean ourselves up or start behaving better. He's inviting us to come and receive life—His life.

You can visit the tombs of Abraham, Buddha, and Mohammed. They are all dead.

Jesus … well, He's alive.

Fear God?

Prior to knowing him, I considered my elementary school principal a big, deep-voiced, scary man. Especially to a small student like me. I had heard stories about his wooden paddle, and you can imagine the fables that were invented. I got in trouble often, and one incident landed me in the principal's office. I don't know about you, but the principal's office was worse than hell, at least in my mind.

I was doomed. I wasn't even worried what my parents would think. I was just wondering whether or not I would die that day—or at least if I'd still be able to feel my bottom. I even heard his paddle had holes in it. Maybe even spikes.

He seemed like Zeus on the other side of his desk. I think lightning struck when I entered. To my surprise, his voice was gentle. He talked to me about what I'd done wrong and what I needed to do to make it right. At this point, I just thought he was buttering me up for the paddle. I don't remember all he said that day, but I do remember this one thing: he reached into his drawer, grabbed a lollipop, and leaned over his big desk to hand it to me.

I deserved some serious punishment. I expected a wearing out, some screaming, and maybe death. But what I got was grace. I got what I didn't deserve. Instead of punishment, I got a lollipop.

We have a twisted view of fearing God. Fear, according to the Bible, is about being in awe of Him, not about being scared of Him (Proverbs 14:26; 1 John 4:18). We think we're in the hands of an angry God. But we're not, no matter what that old preacher tells us. God is our heavenly Father. And He's different from religion because He never gives us what we deserve. He gives us what we don't deserve.

Unlike with religion, we don't have to fear what God will do when we fail. We don't fall away or lose His favor. Nor do we have to fear His punishment. Because of the cross and resurrection, He is always for us. He's not mad at us. The last thing He wants us to do is be scared of Him. He's not a parole officer we have to check in with each month. He's our Father who set us free. And He is leading us to believe that the cross worked. We're forgiven, we're free, and we can fully enjoy Him.

Fear will never lead us to love God or others more. Only grace can do that. Just like the woman in Luke 7 who washed Jesus's feet, those who are forgiven much actually love much. Simply put, when you realize all that has been done for you, the result is more love, not less. Grace, not fear, leads us to be in awe of Jesus. Grace, not fear, leads us to love Jesus.

Jesus didn't die on the cross so you could live your life afraid of Him. Nor did He take your sins away so you would have to face punishment or shame for them. That would be double jeopardy. In America, this means you can't be tried for the same offense twice. God is the same way. He took what you deserved so that you could forever get what He deserved. He died and became your sin, so that you could embrace His love and be confident that you will never face punishment again.

No matter how many times we think we deserve punishment or deserve something bad because of our sin, God's answer will always be the same: "It is finished." God's not handing out condemnation or shame. He will always reach across the desk and hand us what we never deserve— grace.

CHAPTER 8

He's Good

"Oh give thanks to the Lord, for he is good, for
his steadfast love endures forever!"

Psalm 107:1 ESV

God wept.

That was His response when He was headed to see His dead friend, Lazarus—the one the Bible says He loved. Suffering has a way of making God look bad. And our own suffering often leads us to question God's goodness. Not only that, but the suffering in the world can take our breath away and make us wonder, *Where is God in all of this?*

When Lazarus's sisters came to Jesus, they expected Him to do something immediately, like heal their brother. Instead, He gave them a promise: "This illness does not lead to death." He doesn't give them a well-thought-out response to their suffering, but He does give them hope.

I write this chapter with caution because I know many of you are going through, will go through, or have gone through intense suffering and pain. I don't want to give a quick philosophical or theological answer that may not help you. What I've discovered in my suffering is that Jesus, not a well-thought-out response, is our great comfort and hope.

In the midst of our suffering, Jesus doesn't give us a why, He gives us Himself. In Him, we have the hope that suffering and illness do not get the last word, He does. He promises resurrection and life forever. That is what has given me the most peace and comfort in the midst of my pain and suffering.

Every other religion essentially says you get what you deserve. But the whole point of the cross is to destroy any hint of karma. In Jesus, we get what we don't deserve. And even better, we get what Jesus deserves. Christianity is set apart from every world religion because the God of Christianity comes down to suffer for us and with us.

Jesus waited four days before arriving at Lazarus's tomb. This must have felt like a lifetime for Mary and Martha, the sisters of Lazarus. And in the midst of our suffering and pain, it feels the same way. It may be, in our cases, a lifetime of suffering and pain. We're not promised good health or good circumstances. But what we are promised is that Jesus will never forsake us in our pain (Hebrews 13:5).

We don't know why Jesus waited or allowed Lazarus to die. And we don't always know why He allows some things to happen to us—like miscarriage, stroke, divorce, death, loss of a job, starvation, or rape. All these things beg the question, where is Jesus and how could He allow this? Jesus coming to suffer doesn't necessarily give us a specific reason for why He allows some things and doesn't allow others, but it does show us what the reason *isn't*. We can know without a shadow of a doubt that the reason He allows things isn't because He doesn't love us (see Romans 8:38–39).

Mary and Martha sent word to Jesus, saying, "The one you love is sick." John, who wrote this story in his Gospel, called himself the "disciple whom

Jesus loved." He later wrote that "God is love" (1 John 4:8). The one thing John learned from being with Jesus is that Jesus loves people. John knew that it was God's love for us that moved Him, not our love for God. Just because God doesn't do something our way, doesn't mean He doesn't love us.

Many people think that since they can't find a good reason for why suffering exists, there must not be one and there must not be a good God. But just because we can't think of a reason for our suffering doesn't mean there isn't one. Suffering, pain, and evil can be linked to the fall of man. In the beginning, in order for love to exist, God had to give humans a choice to obey Him or disobey Him. To obey or trust Him was to love Him, and to not trust or obey Him was to love something else entirely.

The choice not to trust God set in motion the consequences of sin—evil, suffering, injustice. The reason God gave humans this choice was for the purpose of love to exist. God never wanted to force us to love Him. Suffering and evil are the result of sin and humanity's choice to not trust God. But don't misunderstand me. Your suffering is not because of God's response to *your* sin.

Obviously, there are consequences to our actions and our sin. If we murder someone, we will go to jail. But if you lose your job or someone in your life dies, it's not because you struggle with lying or pride. We live in a broken and fallen world, and bad things just happen. Jesus came down to suffer for us and promised to always suffer with us. That gives us a lot of understanding about what suffering *isn't*.

Jesus is not the creator of our suffering or pain. He allows it in order for us to be free people who can choose to love or not. But He does not cause it. And He is still ultimately in control of this universe. By control, I don't mean a puppeteer. I mean that His plan to restore, redeem, and rescue His people can't be thwarted by us. He is so sovereign that He can give us free choice and still have His plans work out.

Your suffering is not punishment from Jesus. He is not punishing us or shaming us or guilting us or condemning us for our sin (see Romans 8:1). Jesus is not hurling disaster at this world. He wants to save the world, not condemn the world (John 3:17). He wants to draw people by His kindness, not His wrath (Romans 2:14). As believers, He's not against us, He's for us (Romans 8:31).

Your suffering and pain is not from Jesus. He's the One who saves, not the one who inflicts suffering. He's the One who protects us, not causes us pain (2 Thessalonians 3:3; Psalm 46:1). He's not the reason behind our pain; He's our refuge in our pain. He's not the cause; He's the comfort.

Your suffering is not Jesus's trying to teach you a lesson. You (or any sane parent) wouldn't break your two-year-old child's leg to teach them a lesson. God is not breaking you or hurting you or causing you pain in order to teach you a lesson. Nowhere in the New Testament does it say God is breaking us; instead, it says He is building us up (Colossians 2:7; Ephesians 4:12; 2 Corinthians 10:8).

God is not playing good cop/bad cop with us, causing our pain one moment and then comforting us the next. No! He is our great Comforter. He is in the midst of all our suffering, feeling all that we feel. Can we learn and grow from suffering? Sure. But God doesn't need suffering to teach us a lesson. Jesus is a gentle, kind, and loving teacher. And He's not hurting you, breaking you, or harming you in any way. His mission is to build you up and set you free (Colossians 2:6; John 8:32).

Your suffering and pain are not because of your lack of faith either. As children of God, we each have been given faith as a gift (Ephesians 2:8–9; Romans 12:3). We don't need more faith. The Bible says we are complete and have everything we need to live life and live godly (Colossians 2:10; 2 Peter 1:3).

There's a popular teaching out there that says that if you have enough faith, you won't have any problems. But apparently Jesus and the apostles didn't get that message because they were all poor, and they all suffered and died for their faith. Our hope and assurance isn't in overcoming our circumstances; it's in the truth that Jesus has overcome the world.

We exercise faith every day. If you're reading this in a chair, then you have faith the chair will hold you up. But your faith isn't holding you up, the chair is. Our faith isn't what holds us and keeps us, Jesus is. Our faith simply trusts that Jesus will do what He says He will do.

Further, many think that if we buck up and get to work or try harder, then we can "break through" our suffering and experience a better life or better circumstances. This isn't the gospel or Christianity. Instead, everything we need we have in Christ, and our suffering cannot rob what we have in Christ. Being a believer doesn't remove us from suffering, but it does give us God's sufficient grace in the midst of all the pain we go through.

It's worth repeating: your suffering and pain is not because Jesus doesn't love you. Often, our suffering, hurt, and pain causes us to see God through a filter of shame. We think He's distant, irrelevant, or just fed up with us. Not true. He *loves* you. He even *likes* you. He's absolutely delighted in all that you are. His love is independent of your behavior. His love isn't based on your obedience, faithfulness, or commitment to Him. His love and care for you is unconditional, with no strings attached. There's nothing you can do to change God's love for you. *Nothing.*

Further, the Bible gives us clear answers on what Jesus is doing in the midst of our suffering and pain. Christ is in you, through it all. He feels and experiences all the pain that you feel. He's not far off or on the other side. He's in it with you. He loves you. He's comforting you. He cares for you. God causes all things to work together for our good (Romans 8:28), but He doesn't cause all things. He is suffering with you, mourning with you, grieving with you. Holding you. Loving you. And never letting you go.

This is why we need to know that it's okay to be weak. It's okay to be mad. It's okay to doubt. It's okay to grieve.

In all of your pain and hurt and suffering, know this: your connection to Jesus is not about your hold on Him, but His hold on you. Your closeness to Him is not based on your faithfulness to Him, but His faithfulness to you. Jesus's promises to never leave you, always comfort you, and never punish you do not rest on the promises you make to Him, but on the promises He's made to you.

The Bible also tells us what Jesus is doing about our suffering and pain. It started at the cross and through the resurrection. He launched His plan to rid the world of evil and suffering once and for all. Through the cross, He suffered so that one day we would never have to. And through the resurrection, He defeated death and evil, so that one day we can live free from it forever.

Now, He is working everything we go through for our good. How? Sometimes I don't really know. It doesn't always feel like He is in a specific moment. But as I reflect on all the suffering and pain of my life, I can clearly see how He redeemed my suffering. No matter what, we can trust that God wastes nothing. And at His return, He will rid evil once and for all. Evil, sin, and suffering all have expiration dates.

That's what we see in the story of Lazarus. We see Jesus weeping with Lazarus's sisters. He's with them in their pain. He is "I Am." He is always present. He doesn't condemn us for feeling pain and grieving. He feels our hurt and grieves with us. Even though He knew He was about to go resurrect Lazarus, He was with them in the moment. He doesn't get ahead of us or push us to move on. Instead, He's fully present with us. He's patient. He's not in a hurry for you to get over something. In your deepest despair and loneliest moment, Christ is weeping with you.

Time goes by and we don't understand why there's a period of waiting. And Jesus doesn't seek to give us (or Mary and Martha) answers; instead, He gives us Himself fully. Fully present. Fully enough in every moment. Contrary to popular belief, time doesn't heal all things. But Jesus does.

Martha confronted Jesus, saying, "If you had been here, my brother wouldn't have died." Disappointment. Hurt. We all look to Jesus to do something, and when He doesn't, we feel like Martha. There's something about suffering that causes us to question God's presence in our lives and His goodness. You're not alone in your questioning. I've been there. We've all been there.

I used to think suffering robbed me of God's presence, but I now see that God is with me and living in me through it all. If Christ is all I need, then suffering doesn't rob me of anything. It shows me, at a deeper level, all I already have in Christ.

In the next scene, we see Jesus resurrect Lazarus. That is also our hope, that if we believe in Jesus, who is the resurrection and the life, death is not the end of our (or our loved one's) story. If God doesn't exist, then our tears, pain, and suffering are for nothing. But since God does exist, our sorrow will not be wasted. He promises that there will come a day when He will wipe away our tears (Revelation 21:4). No longer will there be any death, mourning, crying, or pain.

Life is painful and hard and tiresome, but Jesus is not. He is gentle and humble with you. That's how Jesus describes His own heart toward you and me (Matthew 11:29). Trusting Him is easy and light, not difficult or tiresome. He's never pointing a bony finger at you but always facing you with open arms. He's always available to you. There are no hoops to jump through to enjoy His life and love.

Trusting in God in the midst of our pain and suffering is not about working or trying. It's not about doing more or working hard. Trusting Jesus is not some burden or law. It's supposed to be easy and light.

It's simply believing. It's believing that He cares for us. In the same way that we care for a hurt body part, Christ cares for us: "For no one ever hated his own flesh, but nourishes and cherishes it, just as Christ also does the church" (Ephesians 5:29–30).

J. R. R. Tolkien asked a question in his book *The Return of the King*: "Is everything sad going to come untrue?" Yes, at Christ's return everything painful and sad will come untrue, and by God's goodness, He restores and works it for our good.

CHAPTER 9

He's Kind

"I am gentle and humble in heart."
Matthew 11:29

I was in fifth grade when I was first made fun of (to my face) for my lazy eye. It was by a group of older boys. I was at my sister's basketball game, and while I was talking to them, one of them remarked, "Who are you looking at?" and "What's wrong with your eye?"

I didn't know what to say. The other boys were laughing. I was embarrassed. It was awkward. In my defense, I thought I was looking at him. But it's one thing for someone to joke about a mistake you made. It's quite another thing for someone to joke about something you can't change.

We all know that being hurtful, abusive, and violent are not okay. It's hard to trust someone like that. And many people have had an experience with God that they thought was similar to my experience with a bully. They believed God was angry, abusive, and unloving.

A common objection to God is the violence we see in the Old Testament. Many think the God of the Old Testament and the God revealed in Christ are different. They say the former was a moral monster, a bully, and unjust.

Just like those funny caricatures we had drawn at the circus, they imagine a sketch of God that exaggerates or completely disfigures His face and character.

Old Testament violence is one of the most difficult topics to address in the Bible. But, as I said earlier, just because we can't think of a good reason for why something happened doesn't mean there isn't one. I'm not God and there are some things I will never understand.

Nonetheless, I do think there is a way forward, and as we will see, God is not some moral monster or bully. Instead, He's a loving God, full of patience and mercy. Since the evidence is clear that God exists and the resurrection happened, I can trust Him. Just like I don't have to understand how a doctor is performing surgery on me, I can trust Him because of the overwhelming evidence of His character.

A Picture, Not a Model

As we step back and look at the entire story of Scripture, we see God protecting His people so that through them He could send Jesus and save the world. Further, we see God judging those who reject Him and do evil. Finally, we see the complete account of Jesus and His victory on the cross and His victory through the resurrection.

It's really easy to create false ideas about God based on some stories in the Old Testament. But when understood in their context and the context of the rest of Scripture, we see that God is and has always been the same.

Whether it's the story of the flood, the destruction of the Canaanites, or any other violence we see in the Old Testament, the first thing to know is that these stories are singular events. They're not the normal way God operates throughout the Bible. The overwhelming theme in the Old

Testament is God's unfailing love and mercy for people who run from Him, reject Him, and want nothing to do with Him. Therefore, the assumption that God was always angry and killing people in the Old Testament is false. These stories are also not moral examples we're meant to follow, nor are they models for us. Instead, they are a part of a larger story, and context will give us clarity to what was actually happening.

God promised Eve and Abraham and His people that through their lineage He would send a Messiah who would save the world. As you read the Old Testament, keep that in mind—that God was protecting the lineage in order to save you and me. He had a plan for Jesus to be born and needed to protect His people so that Jesus would fulfill the thousands of Old Testament prophecies that spoke of His birthplace, lineage, and purpose.

If Old Testament stories of God's judgment on sin bother you, then Jesus's final judgment will bother you more. When Christ returns, He will judge those who reject Him. It's black and white. Those who believe in Jesus will be with Him forever, and those who reject Him will not (Matthew 25:46). God will not force anyone to be with Him.

The penalty for sin is death. We will all die. But those who believe in Jesus are rescued from that penalty and will live forever with Him (Romans 6:23). In Christ, death is a doorway to eternity with Him, not a dead end. And so, in the Old Testament, there were times when God judged those who rejected Him. This is a picture or foretaste of the final judgment.

Whether we recognize it or not, we all want a God who is just. We love justice. We want rape and murder to end. We want justice for those who have been mistreated and oppressed. So does God. And His justice and judgment is an extension of His love. He is ending evil in order to set people free and restore them.

God doesn't mindlessly command the mass killing of people. In every story that speaks of a killing of some people group, there were years of opportunity, sometimes hundreds of years, for those people to turn to God. For example, God gave the Canaanites over four hundred years to turn from their sin. Noah preached to the people in his community for over a hundred years before the flood happened. In addition, the commands to kill weren't always for all the people, but just the soldiers. Many scholars would argue that the purpose of these events was not mass killing, but God's driving out the people from the land and driving out their religion.[34]

God is patient. This is one of the greatest themes throughout the entire Old Testament.

The Canaanites were committing adultery, incest, and bestiality, and sacrificing their children to their gods. They were evil. And God was patient with them, giving them over four hundred years to stop what they were doing. At the same time, He allowed His people to suffer during this time in hopes that the Canaanites would turn away from their sin and to Him.

I find it interesting that many atheists argue that God won't stop evil, but when He does, they also argue against His methods for ending it. So the question is, is God's judgment fair? To me, it's simple. He's patient and kind, wanting all to be saved. But for those who reject Him, He simply gives them what they already knew was coming—death.

I find that many people who pit God's justice against His love have a poor view of justice. It's not unloving to be just. I want to make a point that may seem graphic. If someone were to rape or kill your spouse or child, you would want justice to be served. You love them so much that you believe justice is fair. Furthermore, it is God's holiness and justice, which are expressions of His love, that want to end evil and cancer and all the other wrongs we see in this world.

God's justice isn't only about punishment; it is also restorative. And that's the beauty of the cross. In Christ, we're able to be restored to God because Jesus took the punishment we deserved because of our sins. God offers every human the opportunity to not be punished for their wrongdoings.

I believe God is good and trust that His judgment is fair, and I believe that every single person will have a choice to believe Him or reject Him. He's patient and kind, and I know I can trust His character. Everyone who is in hell is there because they chose to be, and they don't want out. They don't want God. Hell is not a torture chamber for those that end up there. Hell is eternal death and separation from God. God doesn't send anyone to hell. Hell is a choice. And hell is the result of life without God.

Many people wonder why God commanded the killing of children. In the context of those passages, most scholars believe that when the Scripture mentions all the men, women, and children, it's a stereotypical language for "all."[35] Put another way, the language of the Old Testament stories has some "trash talk" and exaggeration built into it—just like a football team would say, "We annihilated them." We see this same type of language used. "We took out the whole city" didn't mean every single person, but instead meant, "We won."

This is why not all the Canaanites were killed. The same can be said about other people groups who were said to be completely killed or destroyed, and then later in Scripture we discover they weren't. Furthermore, when Scripture says that a city was wiped out, it's not a city like we imagine it in today's world. Instead, it was more likely a military base.[36] So the context reveals that when these wars and events happened, it was against soldiers, not innocent people. And many scholars believe every city was given a peace treaty and every person and soldier was given a chance to surrender and turn from their evil.[37]

Also, the biblical text uses the phrase *driving out* or *sent out* more than *destroy* or *annihilate*.[38] Even the words *destroy* and *annihilate* are not meant to be taken literally because they don't mean to kill off every single person; instead, they mean to kill those who fight back.[39] This means women and children and the elderly would have fled as was the normal practice at that time.

As well, like in the flood and other instances, when children and women were killed, we have to remember that God sees things eternally. What might be punishment for some is actually rescue for others. To be born in some of those societies would have meant being offered as a sacrifice, or being raped, abused, or raised as an abuser or murderer. Nonetheless, in all cases, God is judging sin and evil and those who reject Him.

Throughout the Old Testament, we see God fighting for His people. These stories are meant to be a foreshadowing of Jesus's ultimate fight for His people. In all the instances of war in the Old Testament, Israel is the underdog—weaker and often oppressed by their enemy on the battlefield. God, on their behalf, fights for them and wins.

Through the cross and resurrection, Christ, on our behalf, takes upon sin and death and defeats it once and for all. He fights for us. And when He returns, He will end evil and the Evil One once and for all.

God Is Like Jesus

A lie that I'm still tempted to believe is that I'm not enough. One of the reasons stems from that moment I was made fun of for my eye. Shame causes us to believe lies about ourselves and other people.

Shame also causes us to see God through the filter of the lies we believe about ourselves and Him. This happened to Adam and Eve in the garden.

They sinned and the first thing they did was hide from God. They thought He would be angry and kill them. But you know what God did? He pursued them and asked, "Where are you"? Isn't that strange? God knew where they were, but He was seeing where they would identify themselves.

God wasn't after their physical location, but their spiritual one. They were in shame, and when we sin, God is asking us the same question: "Where are you?" Unlike Adam and Eve, although we experience shame and guilt, we're never *in* it. We're always *in* Christ, no matter what. That is why God is constantly reminding us that He is in us and we are in Him.

Jesus came to remove the shame that causes us to hide and question God's goodness. He has promised that He will always be in us and we will always be in Him, no matter the mess we find ourselves in. God is with us in our pain, in our sin, in our shame, and in the darkest moments of our lives.

Jesus came to undo what Adam did. Adam and Eve sinned and hid behind a tree. They were naked and covered in shame, and do you know what Jesus did? He allowed Himself to be crucified, naked, on a tree so that He could conquer sin and shame for us.

If we want to know what God is like, we look to Jesus. Jesus is God, and God is best seen in and represented by Jesus. The New Testament writers were aware of every story in the Old Testament, and what we see throughout the New Testament are descriptions like these: "God is light; in him there is no darkness at all" (1 John 1:5). "God is love" (1 John 4:8). God is "the Father of the heavenly lights, who does not change like shifting shadows" (James 1:17). God is the "Father of mercies and God of all comfort" (2 Corinthians 1:3). God is good (Luke 18:19). God is kind to all (Luke 6:35; Galatians 5:22).

The fruit of the Spirit is what God's character looks like. Love, joy, peace, patience, kindness, goodness, faithfulness, gentleness, self-control. These encompass God's nature and character toward us in every moment. God has always been these things.

If Jesus Christ is the "same yesterday and today and forever" (Hebrews 13:8), and Jesus affirmed the inspiration and authority of the Old Testament by quoting from fourteen of the books of the Old Testament[40], then you and I can trust the Old Testament. I listen to the person who predicted His resurrection and then pulled it off. Further, all the New Testament writers quote the Old Testament and never cast doubt on the Old Testament's inspiration.

Not only that, but I find it comforting and compelling that the New Testament writers knew of the stories we talked about in this chapter. They still wrote these beautiful descriptions about God and didn't feel the need to come to His defense.

We also know that Jesus came to save the world, not condemn it (John 3:17). He came to save, not kill (Luke 9:56). He came to give life, not death (John 10:10). He loves every single person and wants none to perish. Jesus is the exact representation of God's nature and said that "If you've seen me, you've seen the Father" (Hebrews 1:3; John 14:9). Jesus and God the Father are on the same page. It is His kindness that leads humanity to believe in Him (Romans 2:4). The Enemy is the one who "steals, kills, and destroys" (John 10:10), not God.

This means that everything God does is from His goodness and love. Even if we don't understand why or the method God uses to do something, that doesn't mean there isn't a good reason. We can trust that it was loving and good. In all those stories of violence in the Old Testament, sin is the enemy. The story of the Bible is God's loving pursuit of humanity and His ultimate defeat of sin and death for us.

As I mentioned in chapter 2, God treats those who believe in Him differently, not because He has changed but because His covenant with His people has changed. Remember, in the Old Testament, the people were under a covenant of law. Essentially, do your part (obey) and God will do His part (protect and bless). Throughout the Old Testament, God's people continued to disobey and reject God, and yet God continually pursued them with mercy and love. So much so that through the lineage of Israel, God became a man, through Jesus, to save the world.

God hasn't changed. It's in the Old Testament that we discover that God has engraved us on His hands (Isaiah 49:15–16). Zephaniah 3:17 shows us that God takes great delight in us, and Jeremiah 31:20 reveals that God's heart yearns for us. The overarching message throughout the Bible is that God is love.

Thankfully, my older brother was nearby when those boys were making fun of my eye and laughing at me. Bo stood up for me and protected me. Just like God did with Adam and Eve in the garden, Bo came to my rescue. To this day, I still have a deep insecurity about my eyes. I have to force myself to look people in the eyes because I really would rather look away. I fear someone I talk to will ask that question I heard all those years ago.

I'm also learning how to avoid viewing myself or God through shame. I can still get in the trap of viewing God through the lens of my mistakes and fear.

We don't come close to understanding all God does, and we're not supposed to. I used to believe the lies my shame and the world told me about God. I used to think He was an old, angry man in the sky ready to strike me with lightning if I missed a step. But I now see that Jesus is a loving, kind God who gave Himself for me.

Ephesians 2:7 says that "in the ages to come [God] might show the surpassing riches of His grace in kindness toward us in Christ Jesus." Do you see what His plan is for you? He wants to convince you of His kindness and goodness toward you. His plan is to show you the fullness of His grace.

Will you let Him?

CHAPTER 10

He's Love

"God is love."

1 John 4:8

I was eight when our family dog bit me on the leg and went to town on it like it was a turkey leg from the fair. We were playing in the yard, and for whatever reason I became her enemy. Ever since that day, I've had a fear of dogs. Sadly, our dog was put down because of the incident, but what didn't go away was my fear.

Fear has a way of changing our reality. It causes us to lose sight of what is real and true, and can create narratives in our mind that completely control how we live our lives. Fear creates doubts in us, and it causes us to forget the promises and goodness of Jesus. I fear that I am not enough for those around me. I fear that no one really likes me. I fear that maybe God just puts up with me but doesn't really love me.

Fear is often a result of the experiences we've had in life. Maybe it wasn't a dog for you, but a hurtful text, a rejection at work, a break-up, or verbal or physical abuse or worse. All of these can cause us to believe lies. And I used to believe that I could think my way through it or just ignore these lies and fears. Now I realize that the answer is actually to know Jesus's love even more.

Many of us have a fear of trusting God's love. Religion has taught us not to trust in God's goodness. Religion is like my family dog. Sure, religion can die in our life, but many of us still have those thoughts and experiences that hurt us. Many of us still believe things about Jesus that cause us to doubt His love and goodness. If you think you have to earn God's love, you'll spend your entire life performing for Him and never enjoying Him.

John tells us that fear involves punishment and that fear does not exist in God's love (1 John 4:18). He also says that God's unending, perfect love casts out fear. God does the casting out. Our job is to soak in God's love more. Just like with an Epson salt bath, our job is to soak and let the warm salt water do the work.

If what we are hearing or believing about Jesus is producing fear, then it's not from Him. Jesus gives us freedom, not fear. Even though I may still fear and doubt, I now see these things as an invitation to depend on Jesus's love for me even more.

The Unfailing Love of God

Christians are the only people who can describe love the way we do. Reckless, overwhelming, never-ending, unconditional, pure. The list goes on. When we describe God's love, we are at a loss for words because we know that God's love is indescribable. The reason we are the only ones who can describe love this way is because we know Jesus—the One who is love.

In every relationship in which humanity experiences love, it's limited, calculated, and conditional, and usually has an expiration date. We let each other down. We have only so much love to give away. We experience rejection, hate, and love that is faulty from others. In this world, in religion especially, love must be earned; love is achieved through what you do. Jesus's love is given with no expectations. He gives His love to us expecting nothing in return. His love has nothing to do with who we are or what we do. His love is rooted in His character alone.

Being broken up with or cheated on hurts. Whether it happened in seventh grade or last week, it hurts. It stays with you. I still remember discovering that a girlfriend of mine was cheating on me. I felt like the whole relationship was a lie. Romantic relationships had always been difficult for me. Each time I initiated a new one, something would happen to mess it up. The rejection led me to believe that I was not lovable, and that no one would ever want me.

Those experiences coupled with some verbal abuse growing up led me to believe that love was conditional and that there was nothing I could do to get the love and acceptance I was looking for. That caused me to fake it, to wear a mask, to pretend. It cemented my belief that God's love was like the love I experienced on Earth—conditional, out of reach, and not for me.

Marriage changes you. After six months of being married, Grace and I bought a pug. We named him Horace, and I now understand why people love dogs so much. I never thought I'd own a dog, much less fall in love with one this much. To me, Horace is a glimpse of God's work to redeem our worst moments. Love really does remove fear.

Maybe it was a broken home, an abusive parent, or a bad relationship that caused you to believe God's love for you wasn't real. It wasn't until I experienced the unconditional love of God that everything changed for me. Not only did it heal me of past wounds, but it also finally allowed me to be loved and live loved.

Jesus wants us to live in and rest in His love, not earn it. His love is not achieved by doing good works. Religion says, "Work for God's love." God says, "Live from my love." We don't do good works in order to maintain or keep God's love. We do good works *from* God's love for us. God is pleased with us. We are a pleasing aroma to Him (2 Corinthians 2:15). God is delighting in us (Zephaniah 3:17).

Just like a parent who delights in their toddler learning to walk, God is delighting in us in every step. He's a good, good Father who loves to love us. Unlike our fickle love, Jesus's love will never end. John, describing His love for us, says, "[Jesus] loved them to the end" (John 13:1). God's love for us has no expiration date.

Many of us believe that we have to change or act good in order for God to love us. But the good news of Jesus is that it's His love for us that changes us. The focus of our life is not on the love we have for God, but on the great love God has for us.

Jesus often expressed His love through His compassion. All throughout His ministry, He had compassion for those around Him (see Mark 6:34; Matthew 9:36). Every miracle Jesus performed was His way of expressing His love and compassion for others. Our suffering and pain matter to Jesus, and the cross is His ultimate demonstration of the deep love and compassion He has for you and me.

God is not ashamed of us (Hebrews 2:11; 11:16). He's not shaking His head when we mess up and fall short. Instead, He's constantly for us, with a smile on His face. In religion, God's love is always followed with an *if* or *but* or preceded by a *you'd better*. But God's love for you has no strings attached to it. God loves you, period. Jesus's deepest desire is to love you and care for you.

Jesus doesn't need you. He wants you. He doesn't love you so that you can do things for Him. He loves you because He is captivated by you. It's His passion and joy to love you. It's all He wants to do. His heart beats for you. There's never a moment when God won't love you.

Totally Forgiven

Love keeps no record of wrongs (1 Corinthians 13:5). This means God is not up in heaven writing down everything you do wrong. God is living in your heart, reminding you of everything He did right for you and to you. God's love means He's forgiven you of all your sins—past, present, and future. This is one of the greatest ways He expresses His love. If you're looking for God's love, look to the cross. That is where He demonstrated His relentless love for you and me (Romans 5:8). Even when we were against Him, He came for us.

We struggle with Jesus's love because we don't believe He's really forgiven us. We think His love has an expiration date. And that one more sin is going to cause Him to stop loving us. The reason most of us don't believe we are totally forgiven is because, as humans, we have a sin-by-sin system for forgiving sin. We forgive sin when someone asks us for forgiveness. However, Jesus doesn't have a sin-by-sin system for forgiveness.

In the Old Covenant, there was a year-by-year forgiveness system for forgiving sin, which would happen on the Day of Atonement. In Catholicism, church members are required to seek forgiveness based on daily or weekly confession to a priest, and in most Protestant circles, forgiveness is based on our confession of sin to God and asking Him for it each day.

However, the New Testament tells us that God does *not* forgive us sin by sin, confession by confession, or when we ask for it. Instead, Hebrews 9:22 says, "Without the shedding of blood there is no forgiveness." God's requirement for forgiveness is shed blood. Not confession, not going to a priest, and not asking for it daily. This means that blood and nothing else secures forgiveness. Jesus shed His blood, and this brought forgiveness of sins. Since He shed His blood only once and will never shed it again, our forgiveness is a done deal.

God does not have us on a forgiveness payment plan. Nor was the cross a layaway plan, where God purchased some of your forgiveness and you pay for the rest over the period of your life through repentance and confession. He paid for it all. His blood took it *all* away.

When Jesus finished His work, He didn't come to us with an invoice in hand and ask us to pay up. Instead, He handed us the receipt that said, "Paid in full" (see Colossians 2:13–15).

The New Testament is clear: We are made right by His blood (Romans 5:9), ransomed by His blood (1 Peter 1:18–19; Revelation 5:9), cleansed from all sin by His blood (1 John 1:8), freed by His blood (Revelation 1:5), redeemed and forgiven by His blood (Ephesians 1:7), and brought near by His blood (Ephesians 2:13). It is Christ's shed blood, and nothing else, that provides God's forgiveness, cleansing, and presence.

This is God's process or system of forgiving sins. In our world, in order to get something, we must pay for it. If I want gasoline, I must pay for it first in order to receive it. In the same way, in order to have our sins forgiven, blood must be shed as the payment for our forgiveness so that we can receive it. This is God's way. Thus, God forgives sins one time for all time. Hebrews calls this forgiveness "once for all." This means that Jesus offered Himself one time for all sins and His sacrifice is effective for all time. Hebrews 7:27 puts it this way:

> "He has no need, like those high priests, to offer sacrifices daily, first for his own sins and then for those of the people, since he did this once for all when he offered up himself."

Since Jesus is not shedding His blood daily, we are not being forgiven day by day. Jesus, unlike the priests of the Old Testament, does not need to offer Himself repeatedly (Hebrews 9:25), because He has "appeared once for all at the end of the ages to put away sin by the sacrifice of himself" (Hebrews 9:26).

This means that Jesus does not have to die and shed His blood again each day as we sin, because His blood was sufficient for all sins—past, present, and future. If Jesus had to shed His blood again, it would mean His first offering was not sufficient. But we know that what Jesus did worked the first time. It doesn't need to happen again.

As a result of Christ's one offering, Hebrews 10 says we are made holy once for all (v. 10), and "perfected for all time" (v. 14). In the Old Testament, believers could never be made perfect or cleansed (Hebrews 10:1–2). But through Jesus, believers have been perfectly cleansed, made holy, and totally forgiven—forever.

Additionally, we see that God chooses to remember our sins no more: "I will remember their sins and their lawless deeds no more" (Hebrews 10:17). The only reason He can do this is because what Jesus did on our behalf was enough to take away all of our sins. God promises, right now, that He will not hold our sins against us for any reason. This is why when Christ returns, He does not have to deal with our sins again:

"So Christ, having been offered once to bear the sins of many, will appear a second time, not to deal with sin but to save those who are eagerly waiting for him." Hebrews 9:28

When we don't trust that Jesus has forgiven us once and for all, it's kind of like saying we really don't believe His work was enough. We should stop asking Jesus to forgive us again and again when He's made it clear He already has. It is done. If you have placed your faith in Jesus Christ, you are a forgiven person.

There's no such thing as an unforgiven Christian. For this reason, Jesus shouted, "It is finished!" on the cross. In regard to our forgiveness, the work is done. Jesus has closed shop and is now resting at the right hand of God.

Believers now have "confidence to enter the holy place by the blood of Jesus" (Hebrews 10:19). Under the Old Covenant, only the high priest could enter God's presence at a set time. But now, through our total forgiveness, believers can enter God's presence freely. This entry and confidence is spoken of again in Hebrews 4:16: "Let us then with confidence draw near to the throne of grace."

The only reason we can have confidence to enter God's presence is that we are forgiven and cleansed. To say that a holy God would allow unforgiven and imperfectly cleansed people in His presence is to denigrate the holiness of God. God is perfectly holy and thus makes us perfectly holy in order for us to be together with Him. This is why the New Testament tells us over and over that we are saints, holy, sanctified, and righteous (see 1 Corinthians 1:2; 6:11; 2 Corinthians 5:21; Romans 1:7).

The New Testament is clear that forgiveness is a completed work. Our redemption and forgiveness have been secured. If we believe in Jesus, then we are forgiven and we are redeemed. We are not waiting or hoping for forgiveness from Jesus; we already have it. To be redeemed means to be forgiven. You cannot have one without the other. I don't wake up each day and ask my wife to marry me again, because our marriage is already true. We got married one time for all time. In the same way, we're redeemed and forgiven once and for all:

> "We have redemption, the forgiveness of sins." Colossians 1:14

> "In him we have redemption through his blood, the forgiveness of our trespasses." Ephesians 1:7

Combining the truth of Colossians 2:13 that says, "God made [us] alive together with him, having forgiven us all our trespasses" (ESV), and that of 1 John 2:12 that says, "Your sins are forgiven for his name's sake" (ESV), we realize the message is clear: we are forgiven people. The work is done. We don't have to do anything for God to forgive us. Our sins are forgiven.

As I'll talk about more in chapter 14, knowing we are completely forgiven doesn't lead us to sin more, nor does it give us a "license to sin." Those who claim we need to confess or ask for forgiveness could have that same license. "If I sin, I can just ask God to forgive me."

Second Peter 1:9 actually tells us that ungodliness is a result of forgetting our forgiveness. Here's why: when I don't believe I'm forgiven, my focus is on sin and shame and guilt, which just leads to more sin, more shame, and more guilt. In contrast, total forgiveness doesn't lead us to sin more; it actually enables us to be set free from shame and guilt and to focus on Jesus, the Author and Perfecter of our faith.

Let's repent each day (change our mind), let's confess our sins to one another and to God if we want, but let's do it knowing God has already fully forgiven us.

Jesus is better than religion because His love isn't based on our performance. Jesus loves us independent of what we do for Him. Jesus loves us because it's who He is. Jesus is leading us to believe that the truest thing about who we are is that we are loved and cared for by Him and we have done nothing to deserve it.

God keeps no record of your wrongs. He doesn't have graph charts of your prayer and Bible study time. He isn't busy editing your highlight video of sinning so that He can bring it up when you reach heaven (He remembers your sins no more, according to Hebrews 10:17). God has no strings attached. No secret agenda. He just wants to love you and delight in you!

A popular message in many churches today is all about what we need to do to get our minds and heart dedicated and committed to God. But our assurance and security is not found in our dedication and commitment to God. Our assurance is found in how God's loving heart is always dedicated and committed to us.

For God so loved … you!

PART 3:

BETTER THAN SIN

"You will make known to me the way of life; in Your presence is fullness of joy; in Your right hand there are pleasures forever."
Psalm 16:11

"For a day in Your courtyards is better than a thousand elsewhere. I would rather stand at the threshold of the house of my God than live in the tents of wickedness."
Psalm 84:10

CHAPTER 11

He Saves

"He rescued me, because He delighted in me."

Psalm 18:19

D o you remember falling in love for the first time? I do. Falling in love with Grace was the greatest thing that has ever happened to me. I find her beauty, humor, knowledge, and love for people so attractive. You may not believe this, but in college I prayed that my wife would be named Grace. I figured if God's grace is so amazing, then surely a girl named Grace would be too.

Grace loves to remind me that she loved me first, but that's a story for her to tell. She has brought so much healing and comfort and joy into my life that I never knew anyone, especially me, could experience. I tell people that she is "God's wink" to me, because I was always searching for love but had never found it before Grace. She is God's way of telling me, "I got you, bro."

Before Grace, I didn't realize how much I needed her. Struggling with the lie that I was not worthy of love, I always thought I wasn't attractive enough or good enough for someone to truly love me. Grace has this remarkable ability to give you her full attention and make you feel like you're the only person in the world and that nothing else in the world matters in that moment. She also has a way with words that encourages me and makes my fears and struggles fade away.

Grace doesn't follow me, and I don't follow her. We're in relationship together. We're married. She would never describe our relationship in this way. Nor would I. And I don't think the best way to describe our relationship with Christ is as followers. We're in relationship with Him. The Bible says we're married to Him. The disciples followed Jesus, but we have Christ in us. We have something better than just following Jesus. We have a living, breathing relationship with Christ in us every moment of every day.

What have you done for God lately? Are you living your life for God? These questions imply that we live our lives separated from God, like He's the King in the palace and we are servants in the field. But the New Testament is clear: everything we do is "in Christ" or "in Him." Every step we take, we take with Christ in us.

Jesus's mission was to set us free from the bondage of sin and that ache we feel for something more satisfying than sin (Luke 4:18). Sin over-promises but under-fulfills every single time. However, a relationship with Jesus exceeds your expectations every single time. Religion is about following the rules. Jesus is about relationship. Religion and every other world system is about what you can do. Religion requires you to work hard to achieve what is promised. In work life, working harder is the only route to success. We work in order to accomplish, and we do in order to be.

Jesus doesn't demand; He invites. He doesn't coerce us; He woos us with His love. Jesus doesn't invite us to join a country club where we get a membership, pay a fee, go to some meetings, and then enjoy some perks. He invites us to a life-changing relationship. We're not asked to simply buy into some belief system; instead, it's more like falling in love with Him. That's Christianity.

Jesus doesn't want us to just "behave." He isn't trying to get bad people to act good. Instead, Christianity is about giving dead people (that's all of us) life. The Bible says that we are all dead and in need of life (Ephesians 2:1–8). Have you noticed that there is a deep longing in everyone? An ache. A hunger. For something better than the world can offer.

Without food or water, we will die. This is why God built hunger and thirst into our bodies—to remind us to eat and drink. In the same way, all of us have a hunger and thirst that can only be satisfied by our Creator.

Lying, stealing, cheating, pride, gossip, lust. None of these things can give life—not even wealth or fame. Just check Instagram or Facebook and you'll see another miserable celebrity. Nothing the world offered worked for me, and my guess is it's not working for you. How do you know? Do you still feel empty, like you want or need more, even after a great accomplishment? Sin isn't just the bad stuff we do. Sin is anything that robs us of experiencing Christ.

For me, sin never was the answer, no matter how hard I tried for it to be. Every night I would still lay in bed with the same ache: *I'm not enough. I need more.* I longed for something, anything, to fill the longing to be loved and wanted.

The deepest need of the human heart is to be loved and accepted. We all desire to be wanted, valued, and loved. The good news of Jesus is that in Him, we're totally loved and unconditionally accepted—no matter what. If our greatest need was more money, God would have sent us a financial guru. If it was more knowledge, God would have just sent us a teacher. Since our greatest need was life, God sent us Himself.

Jesus isn't asking you to be "good enough." He extends the invite to us all, no matter our past. There's no fee to pay, no class to take, and nothing for us to do—except accept His invitation. That's what it means to be saved by grace. It means there's nothing you can do to earn your salvation and there's nothing you can do to lose it. It's a free gift. God is described as being "rich in mercy" (Ephesians 2:4). It's His passion to drown us in His mercy and love.

We have all sinned and fallen short of God's standard. That's why Jesus came to rescue us. The penalty for our sin was death. So Jesus came and took our sin and the penalty for our sin by dying, so that we could be free from the penalty. But He did more. Through His resurrection, He also set us free from the power of sin as well by giving us His life. As a result, we have unhindered access to Him.

The apostle Paul tells us that we are saved by God's grace alone, not works (Ephesians 2:8–9). This is Paul's way of saying that we're saved by Jesus. We're not saved by a doctrine or piece of paper; we're saved by a Person. We were lost and He found us. We were blind and He came and gave us sight. We were dead and He came and gave us life—His life.

Salvation isn't just a ticket to heaven. When Jesus saves us, He forgives us for all sins, and gives us an identity that is based on His opinion, a freedom that cannot be shaken, and His life inside of us, no matter what.

The Mobster Named Zac

Luke 19 tells the story of a rich, well-dressed mobster named Zacchaeus. He was infamous—for being a tax collector. Not just any tax collector but the chief tax collector. He collected taxes from his own people for the Roman government and filled his pockets by skimming from his fellow Jews. He was one of the most hated men in town.

God doesn't have a scale for bad people. What God sees are people who are in need of Him. So your mess isn't too big for God. No matter your past, your present, or any failure you've made, God meets you exactly where you are. Not only that, but nothing disqualifies you from being loved or used by God. Abraham was a liar; Rahab was a prostitute; and Paul, Moses, and David were murderers and wrote a lot of the books in the Bible. God loves meeting your mess with His mercy.

Back to Zacchaeus. One day, he wanted to get a look at Jesus as He came through town and, since he was short, he climbed up a tree to catch a glimpse. To his surprise, when Jesus walked by, He looked up, called Zacchaeus by name, and said, "I want to come hang out with you."

A few years ago, I went to watch one of my favorite communicators in person. After the event, there was a long line to meet and talk to him. Before the event, we had communicated on Facebook a few times, but we weren't best friends or anything. I was nervous and excited to meet my hero for the first time. Finally, I was next in line. Once he finished with the person in front of me, he looked at me as if I was the only person in that large auditorium, and said, "Zach! Are you kidding me?" He gave me a hug and said, "You're such a young hero of mine."

Wait, hold up. My hero was telling me I'm a hero? Say whaaat? I was blown away by how he made me feel like I was the only one in the room. Sure, I was a super fan, but who does that? There's no greater feeling than to feel like you matter—and not only that but to be called by name. One of the first names God is given in the Bible is *El Roi*, which means "the God who sees me." He sees you. He knows everything about you, and He loves you.

Anyway, Jesus really did go to Zacchaeus's house to hang out with the guy most of the people considered the worst person in town. People often accused Jesus of being a drunk and glutton because he constantly hung out with drunks and gluttons. Jesus was fun to hang out with. People enjoyed His company. Zacchaeus was pumped to have Jesus come over. I don't know about you, but when people randomly invite themselves to my house, I'm usually less than excited. This tells you something about the nature of Jesus.

Many of us picture Jesus like the pope or some high religious figure. No offense to the pope, but I don't think it would be much fun to hang out with him for too long. Jesus isn't like that. There was something about Jesus's personality that made Him seem like He was a normal, down-to-earth guy—just one of them. That's one of the things we sometimes forget about Jesus. He was both fully God and fully human.

We don't know what Jesus and Zacchaeus talked about. We can assume they ate a meal, maybe shared some jokes, talked about their week, and so on. What we do know is that everything changed for Zacchaeus after that visit. The Bible doesn't give the details, but I like to imagine that for the first time, Zacchaeus was heard and loved. Zacchaeus was looking into the eyes of God and didn't experience rejection and shame, but rescue and salvation. Jesus knew everything about Zacchaeus. He knew he was a cheat and a thief, but He wasn't there to prosecute or accuse. He was there to save.

My favorite modern-day picture of Jesus is of Him laughing and dancing with children. How do you picture Jesus? Is He mad? Sad? Disgusted and frustrated? Believe it or not, He's got a smile on His face. He dances with joy over you (Zephaniah 3:17)! It's the kindness and tender heart of God that leads us to repent and trust Him (Romans 2:4).

Zacchaeus told Jesus that he would give half his wealth to the poor and repay four times the amount that he cheated people on their taxes. Wow.

That's what God's love does. Jesus didn't have to give Zacchaeus a list of what to do and not do. His love caused Zacchaeus's heart to change, and the behavior followed that. I think the Bible doesn't tell us what Jesus and Zacchaeus talked about because it wasn't about what was said that changed Zacchaeus; it was about who he was with.

Jesus—not devotion, a principle, a good deed, or effort—changed Zacchaeus. Jesus—not a moral handbook, rules, or commandments—caused Zacchaeus to right his wrongs. Jesus is after heart transformation, not behavior modification. He will never use shame or guilt or manipulation to win someone's heart. It's His kindness that leads us to repentance (Romans 2:4).

I used to think that if I tried hard enough, I could get God's attention, and that it was up to me to reach God and impress Him and get Him to save me. Just like Zacchaeus, we all want to do more and try harder in hopes that Jesus will see us and like us. But that's not what saved Zacchaeus, and that isn't what saves you and me. It was Jesus who saw Zacchaeus. Jesus who invited Zacchaeus. And Jesus who saved and changed Zacchaeus forever.

Patient, kind, loving, fun, generous, good, happy, enjoyable—that's Jesus. Just a few moments with Jesus changed Zacchaeus. And the more we come to understand the heart of Jesus, the more it transforms us too.

A New Design

Grace and I were driving to a speaking event I had a few hours from where we live. We enjoy going on trips together, and I love taking Grace when I go speak. She drove the last hour so I could finish preparing for the message and get a little nap in before I spoke. About thirty minutes out, we realized the gas tank was empty. We were not in a major city. We were in the desert. At least it felt that way.

Traveling down a two-lane highway in the middle of nowhere in Texas, we found no gas stations in sight. We plugged on, hoping and praying my car would make it. We didn't encounter ANYONE, not even a car or a house or a windmill or a cow. Nothing.

I knew my car could drive for about twenty to thirty miles on empty, so I thought we had a chance. Oh, and I forgot to mention, there was no cell service either. On top of that, I had been taught that if you're on time, you're late. I hate being late to anything. I was a little stressed.

We finally reached the small town where I was to speak and pulled into the first gas station. We both thought it was sketchy. No one was there, but it had fuel pumps. I hopped out to put a few gallons in my car to get us down the road to a better station.

I couldn't believe we made it. We survived. My car did it!

Then, as we pulled into the next gas station to get more gas and some coffee, my car started acting weird. The steering wheel got tight and I could barely accelerate, but I just assumed it was because we were low on gas. I filled up, got my coffee, and hopped back in the car.

But it wouldn't start. I turned the key in the ignition, and nothing. Again and again and again. Nothing. I called the event coordinator to tell her I was right down the road and my car wouldn't start. No answer. Called again. Nothing.

So Grace and I grabbed my bag and walked the rest of the way to the event. As we like to say, we made a memory.

As it turned out, I'd accidently put DEF in my car at the sketchy gas station. DEF is for diesel engines, and when you put it in a gas engine like mine, it messes up the whole engine and fuel lines and everything. My car is not designed to run on DEF; it's designed to run on gasoline.

As believers, we're designed to trust in Jesus to meet our needs. Sin is like DEF. We're not designed for it. We're designed to live from the life of Jesus. And through faith in Christ, we find our compatibility with Him. This means that we crave what God has for us. Commands and instruction from God are not have-tos but now want-tos.

Jesus gives us a new heart and He lives inside that heart. Since Christ is our source and we have new hearts, we're designed for something better than sin. We're designed to trust Jesus and express Him in all that we do. Just like a water hose connected to a water source, we find our purpose and meaning when we're trusting Christ.

Paul explains our design in Ephesians 2:10: "For we are His workmanship, created in Christ Jesus for good works." You're God's workmanship, or masterpiece. You've been created or designed for good works. God did not save you and then recreate you as somebody who is sinful. He made you a new creation who was designed for good works, not sin.

As we learn what to do, we realize that life is not about keeping the rules; instead, it's about trusting that Jesus knows what is best for us. He knows what will give us peace and joy and happiness, and He shows us that DEF (sin) won't ever work for us. It will never fulfill or make us happy.

Contrary to popular teaching, you're not designed for sin. That's why when you sin, you feel regret. As a new creation, you discover you no longer want to sin. You're designed for obedience and love because God has made you loving and obedient from your heart (Romans 5:5; 6:17).

We often think that the way to stop sinning is to just stop. But haven't you noticed that your will power isn't enough? The answer is actually relationship with Jesus. It's when we know Him and live our lives rooted and grounded in Him, that sin loses its appeal and we begin to trust Jesus for everything. This is exactly why Paul tells us in Colossians 2:6 to continue to live our lives the same way we began our relationship with Christ, by trust alone: "Therefore as you have received Christ Jesus the Lord, so walk in Him."

Being saved by Jesus changes us from the inside out. We start an adventure of knowing Christ, and through knowing Him we discover what we are created for. We long for meaning and purpose, and in Jesus we discover those answers. Along the way, we get a friendship that is unshakeable and unbreakable.

Next, let's look at how Jesus fulfills us.

CHAPTER 12

He Fulfills

"I am the bread of life; whoever comes to me shall not hunger,
and whoever believes in me shall never thirst."

John 6:35

I was on a plane recently when I finally listened to the long talk the flight attendants give. Part of the speech deals with the oxygen mask that comes down from the ceiling. They tell you to put your own mask on before you help others put theirs on. But this went against what I'd always been taught.

I always believed I needed to focus on others more than myself, thinking that this was "true humility" and what God wanted. You know what happened? I was left worn out, tired, and broken. It's not that thinking of others is bad, but when we neglect ourselves, we can't love others.

Jesus gave us a new direction and instruction. He said to "love one another; just as I have loved you" (John 13:34). Receiving His love first is what He wants us to do. The first step to finding fulfillment is to receive God's love. Jesus gave us a blueprint for a fulfilled life, and it starts by receiving His love and then expressing His love. Are you being kind to yourself? Or are you focusing more on your job, your failures, or even your kids rather than the tender love of Jesus?

You can't earn His love. It's a free gift. You can't lose His love. It's unconditional. You can't do anything to make Him love you more or less. His love for you is rooted in His character, not your choices. Jesus loves to love you. This is not the marketplace. God doesn't exchange His love for our good behavior. His love for us is constant, never changing, and is not based on what we do or don't do. Even when we fail, His love is unfailing.

God loves you as much as He loves Jesus (see John 17:23). John 1:18 says that Jesus is in the Father's "arms" or on His "chest" and has made God known to us. The night before the crucifixion, John, the "disciple whom Jesus loved," was found leaning back on Jesus's chest (John 13:23). Jesus came to put you back on Dad's chest and for you to know His tender love for you. He wants you to hear His heart beat for you. Jesus wants you to know His unfailing love for you.

I was wrong about humility and my assumption of what God wanted. I now know that He designed us to receive from Him first before we can do anything to help others. Only when we put our mask on and get oxygen can we then help others put theirs on. Put another way, only when we let ourselves receive God's love can we help others receive His love.

Finding Fulfillment and Purpose

I hate working out. It was all I did from middle school through college. Don't get me wrong. It enabled me to eat whatever I wanted and not look like a sumo wrestler. But after I finished playing college football, I stopped going to the gym. Like most people do, I tried to get back to the gym or do those at-home workouts, but nothing worked for me. I also don't like healthy food. Pizza and brownies are my love language.

One day, my mom called me up and said, "Zach, I think you look good, but ..."

Now, I love my mom more than anyone can love their mom. She is the best mother in the world. And in our family, we are direct and blunt and don't always consider each other's feelings. When I heard the word *but*, I knew it couldn't be good. (FYI, if you're trying to get a girlfriend or boyfriend, never say *but* after "I think you look good." Come to think of it, it is never a good idea.)

She continued, "I think you need to start working out again. I will pay for the first six months of your gym membership."

I laughed and told her that I would find a gym. I knew her heart and trusted that she wanted what was best for me. After joining a gym and working out consistently four times a week for nine months, I lost over fifteen pounds and felt great about myself and my body. My energy increased, and I actually kind of liked working out. I was even eating less and making better decisions about food, which meant a little less brownies and pizza.

Then coronavirus hit.

At first, I thought, *Oh, this is good. I'll give myself a little break and it will be fine and I'll just work out from home.* The first Monday I woke up at my normal time, got my running shoes on, and headed out the door to do my first at-home run. I ran a mile, called it good, and felt accomplished. But then Tuesday hit, and I didn't want to run. And well, let's just say I don't have the self-discipline to work out from home.

I didn't work out for three months. I don't know why, but I just had no motivation to work out from home. I can wake up and go to a gym and workout, but I can't from home.

During the coronavirus at-home time, I ate more, not less. When you're working from home and not working out, why not eat? I put on some more weight and started feeling bad about myself. And what's crazy, I knew I was eating too much and I would still keep eating. What's another cookie or a few more bites when you already feel fat, right?

I am good at not changing. It's a lot easier to keep doing something I'm used to than to change and do something else. Even if the thing I'm doing is making me feel miserable. Many of us have been living unfulfilled lives. We know it's not healthy, but we keep doing it. We scroll through social media, and we wish we were like the Joneses down the street or like that influencer or Instagram model. We believe that one more purchase or a better job or a change of circumstance is going to bring us happiness and fulfillment. That's partly why studies show that two-thirds of people are not happy.[41]

We know that Jesus promises to be enough, but day to day it doesn't feel like He is. One way you can define sin is anything that seeks to fulfill you that isn't Christ. Put another way, sin is when we look to anything other than Jesus to meet our needs. We've believed the lie that sin is better than Christ. Even though we know it isn't, we keep choosing it over and over again. We feel miserable. But what's another sin if you think you're a bad person?

We've bought the lie that sin is all that stuff we want to do but aren't allowed to. But as we will discover, as new creations, sin is the last thing we want to do. We're actually designed to let Christ meet our needs and fulfill us.

Jesus said that He is the bread of life (John 6:35). This means that He sustains and fulfills us. Just like we receive food to sustain us, once we receive Jesus, He gives us His eternal life. He has promised us that He will meet every one of our needs (Philippians 4:19). Not only that, but He wants us to be happy, not miserable. If God is happy, and He is, then He wants His children to be happy too.

I can already hear the religious saying, "No! God wants us to be holy, not happy!" I don't think we have to pit the two against each other. If I am reading my Bible right, God has already "made us holy once and for all" (Hebrews 10:10). The good news is meant to bring us joy, not sadness (see Luke 2:10). As we trust Him, our behavior will be holy because that's who we are now in Him.

When Grace and I were planning our wedding, the guest list was probably the most stressful thing for us to do. Because of the size of the venue and the limitations due to COVID-19, we couldn't invite everyone. It was difficult to decide who to put on the list and who to keep off. We had to literally go through it and compare people. I know, that sounds terrible, but if you've ever planned a wedding, you know what I'm talking about. Chances are, if we thought you were more fun, you made the list.

Jesus got invited to a wedding. The bride or the groom made sure that He was on the list. It was one of the first things Jesus did after He started His ministry, so the bride and the groom didn't invite Jesus because He was the popular guy who did miracles. Jesus hadn't even performed a miracle yet. They invited Jesus because He was fun and cool to be around. Jesus wasn't the "holier than thou" guy. He lightened up the party. He was liked. People enjoyed Him.

The story is found in John 2, and it only gets better. After the wine ran out, Jesus performed His first miracle—turning water into wine. It wasn't the cheap wine you buy on sale at the grocery store; it was the best wine of the wedding. The Bible says that He turned six thirty-gallon water jars into wine. That's about a thousand bottles of wine!

I think this story is recorded for a few reasons. One, it illustrates that Jesus is fun to be around. He's not like an awkward coworker you hate hanging out with. And two, this story is a picture of God's economy. He gives us all of Himself, with no strings attached. There's no carrot on a stick. Jesus turned the water into wine and blessed the wedding because of who He is. And He's not withholding anything from us either.

To believe that Jesus can fulfill us and meet our needs, we need to first believe that He's actually fun to be around and that He wants to be around us. We will only receive His love if we trust Him, and we need to know that He will never hold back from us. Over and over throughout His life, Jesus gave and gave and gave. His love for you is an unending river that will never run dry.

When I believe that sin is better and that Jesus doesn't want me to be happy or fulfilled, it's easy for me to choose sin and keep feeling miserable. But when I believe that Jesus is better than sin and that He wants to fulfill me, I can choose what He wants. When I was working out, it was easy to make better choices about my food and it gave me a healthy view of myself. In the same way, Jesus wants us to practice trusting Him. As we do that, it will be easier for us to make better choices in our thoughts and behavior.

That seems like a paradox. How do you practice trusting God? It's one thing to believe that Jesus can fulfill you. It's another thing to apply it to your life. It's one thing to believe working out is good for you; it's another thing to actually work out. But you're not alone in this. Christ is in you! Christ is "directing your hearts into the love of God" (2 Thessalonians 3:5) He's given you faith as a gift (Romans 12:3), and it's His love that compels us (2 Corinthians 5:14). So, as you learn to trust Christ in every moment, recognize that "He who calls you is faithful; he will surely do it" (1 Thessalonians 5:24).

As we receive God's love, we naturally love others. It's an overflow. And as we love others, we experience the love God has for us as He expresses His love through us. Haven't you noticed that when you make others happy, you become happy? When you encourage someone, you are encouraged as well. Don't worry, the timing is up to God. He has prepared the good works for us; our job is to just be available. One study revealed that when people thought about giving money away or about doing good for others, it triggered the part of the brain that is associated with happiness. Loving others actually triggers dopamine, the chemical that makes us feel good, in our brain.[42]

That's why we can be fulfilled no matter the circumstance we find ourselves in. Jesus gives us hundreds of ways to love others. He doesn't order us to do them so we can earn His love or blessings. It's part of our design! We don't have to love and serve others in order to please God. He's already pleased (2 Corinthians 2:15). We're simply letting God be God in and through us.

You have everything you need to live a fulfilled life (2 Peter 1:3). You are blessed with every spiritual blessing (Ephesians 1:3). You don't need more of Jesus, and you're not lacking anything (Colossians 2:10). Since Christ is in you, you have all you need. Jesus isn't dangling fulfillment on a stick in front of you and asking you to try harder or be better in order to achieve it. He is fulfillment, and He is inviting us to trust Him in every moment.

When we trust Jesus, we express Jesus, and as we do, we find fulfillment. Jesus is the door, but He is also the room. He promises us abundant life, here and now. But abundant life is not a perfect set of circumstances. No, abundant life is Jesus Himself. Jesus is not a means to an end; He is the means and the end. He is the journey and the destination. He is everything from start to finish.

In order to fully embrace that truth, I have to stick with it. It's a little like working out. I have to practice believing that in Christ, I am loved, accepted, new, righteous, and enough. When I do, it's easier for me to say no to sin and to choose thoughts and actions that fit with who I am. When you hear the lie in your head that says you're not enough, you have the choice to entertain that thought or to counter it with the truth that "God says I'm enough."

I have to keep repeating that truth to myself. Over and over. Paul calls this renewing our mind (Romans 12:2) and taking every thought captive (2 Corinthians 10:5). Put another way, God wants us to replace lies and false beliefs with the truth about Him and who we are in Him.

We live in an instant gratification society. We want things now, and we usually get them. Just like with a microwave, you pop your food in and in less than a few minutes, you have a meal. But replacing old thoughts with new thoughts is like using a crockpot, not a microwave. It takes time. It isn't instant. In the same way that you can't go to the gym one time and expect instant results. Or you can't go one time and expect for that to be enough for the rest of your life. That's like our mind; we have to constantly renew it to the truth of God's Word.

Christ in you enables you to both trust Him and make healthy choices. He's given you the power to choose Him and not choose sin. So what if, instead of choosing bitterness, you chose joy? What if in the morning when you wake up, instead of complaining, you gave thanks? Jesus tells us to work out all that He's worked in us (Philippians 2:11–12). He promises that He's at work in us (v. 13). So, as we work out and renew our minds to what God has told us, we enjoy what God has done and is doing in us.

We find joy and happiness and fulfillment as we let Christ live through us. We are fully dependent upon Him, and yet it feels like we are just living. Since we are in union with Christ, my being myself and Christ living through me feels the same. The New Testament gives us over fifty things we can do for one another, such as forgiving one another, encouraging one another, accepting one another, praying for one another, and serving one another. As we love and express Christ, we're not always going to feel like doing it. But the more I let Christ live through me, the more I recognize that I've been created for this (see Ephesians 2:10).

We need one another. When God created Adam, He said it wasn't good for him to be alone. Why didn't God tell Adam, "You have Me! You don't need a partner!"? Because God created us for community. Since we find fulfillment by receiving God's love and by expressing His love, that primarily happens in a community of believers. But not exclusive to that.

It's part of your design to give away love like you're made of it. Because you are! God has poured out His love into your heart (Romans 5:5), and you have an incorruptible love for Him (Ephesians 6:24). I'm not saying it's easy to love the difficult child, irritating friend, or prideful neighbor, but you're not alone. God is making your love "increase and overflow" for others (1 Thessalonians 3:12). Each time you love, you get the awesome opportunity to experience Christ through you!

Many of us have been taught to make sure our hearts are "right with God." We're constantly inspecting ourselves and our motives. But you've been made right with God once and for all (Romans 5:1). Your heart is new and right and your motives are already godly. If you're going to inspect anything, inspect the finished work of the cross and resurrection.

If you're looking to make a difference or be a part of something bigger than yourself, it doesn't mean you have to cross the ocean. It can happen in your house or dorm, with your literal next-door neighbor, or at work. We get the awesome opportunity each day to just love those around us with no agenda.

CHAPTER 13

He Teaches

"For the grace of God has appeared, bringing salvation to all people,
instructing us to deny ungodliness and worldly desires and to live
sensibly, righteously, and in a godly manner in the present age."

Titus 2:11–12

I wonder why most of us can remember every elementary school teacher we had but we can hardly recall the teachers we had in middle and high school? Perhaps it's because our elementary teachers were involved, they cared, and they were after relationship.

Christianity is not about following a dead religious teacher. Christ has made us His dwelling place. We're not left to figure this life out on our own. He is fully available to us and is involved with every aspect of our life.

Sin is burdensome. We often let the mistakes of our past cripple our present life. Shame, guilt, regret—we carry them with us as if they are consequences we deserve. Maybe we think Jesus will treat us like children with some spiritual version of a timeout, detention, or spanking. We might even imagine a heavenly version of karma: Do good and God will bless you; do bad and God will not be kind to you.

We think we need to work on our sin. We think it's our job to fight our way out of our sin struggle. And we think that Christ in us is not practical for day-to-day life. Many in the church talk about what we need to do for Jesus; rarely do we talk about what Jesus is doing for us each day. The church is full of teaching on how we need to live for Jesus, but we have missed the real message that not only is Jesus living through us, but He is also living in us each day as our Teacher and Helper. Christ in you is not symbolic. He's really in you, every moment.

Jesus teaches us a lot about how to live life, but He also teaches us about Himself. This is what we need to lean in to—not principles for daily living, but a Person. Not rules that have the appearance of wisdom, but the reign of Christ and His wisdom in our hearts. Not doctrine, but our heavenly Dad.

When we read about the life of Jesus, we discover a God who says He's like a shepherd who will leave the ninety-nine in order to rescue the one. He tells us a story of a Father who gives His son His finest robe, places a ring on his finger, and throws Him a party right after the son just returned home from squandering his inheritance. Jesus demonstrates how He reacts to our sin with the story of the woman caught in adultery—not by shaking His head in disgust, but by dismissing her accusers, picking her up, telling her she is not condemned, and empowering her to go and sin no more.

He's that good. Jesus is not far off or distant. He's united to us. He's promised to never leave, no matter how messy life gets. The New Testament reveals to us that Jesus teaches us one way and one method—through grace. It is the grace of God, not fear or manipulation or wrath, that teaches us to say no to sin and to live godly (Titus 2:12).

Grace from Beginning to End

Jesus gives us a picture of what living with Him looks like in Matthew 11:29–30: "Take my yoke upon you and learn from me, for I am gentle and humble in heart, and you will find rest for your souls. For my yoke is easy and my burden is light" (NIV). In this context, the yoke represents teaching or lifestyle. Jesus invites us to learn from how He lives.

He is gentle and humble. He isn't threatening that we'd better behave. He's not in a hurry with our behavior. He's not whipping us when we do wrong. He's not going to fly off the handle. He's patient, kind, keeps no record of our wrongs, is not easily angered, and always protects us (see 1 Corinthians 13).

Jesus's teaching and lifestyle is summed up by one word—grace. He's the full expression of both grace and truth (John 1:14, 17). Some say we need to balance grace and truth. But grace is the truth that will set us free.

Grace is God's favorite word. It's used over one hundred times in the New Testament. It's the Bible's way of describing God. God is the "God of all grace" (1 Peter 5:10), grace is Jesus (Titus 2:11), grace is the good news of what Christ has done (Acts 20:24). We are: saved by grace (Ephesians 2:8; Titus 2:11), taught by grace (Titus 2:12), standing in grace (Romans 5:2), strengthened by grace (2 Corinthians 12:9; 2 Timothy 2:1), forgiven and redeemed by grace (Ephesians 1:7), made right by grace (Romans 3:24), empowered by grace (1 Corinthians 15:10), equipped by grace (2 Corinthians 9:8), called by grace (Galatians 1:3), righteous by grace (Galatians 2:21), favored by grace (Ephesians 1:6), and loved and comforted by grace (2 Thessalonians 2:16).

It's not fear that teaches us. It's not the fear of getting caught or getting in trouble that teaches us. That's not how God works. Jesus takes us by the hand and teaches us how to live and how to say no to the burden-heavy, shame-filled, weary path of sin. God has a way of teaching us that is unlike any way we've ever been taught. It's not through shame, it's not through guilt, and it's not through a reward system. It's through relationship with Christ in us.

It's not the law that teaches us. It's not the Old Testament commands or any law we put on ourselves. Jesus is not using a "thou shalt" system to make us obey or learn. We're under grace, not the law (Romans 6:14). By His grace, sin no longer has control over us. Sin actually thrives under law (Romans 7:8), but by God's grace we are released from the law and set free to discover that our heart's desire is Him (Ephesians 6:24). The way forward is by trusting in Christ, not striving. It's not about trying to defeat sin or overcome temptation; it's about trusting in Jesus, who has already defeated sin and who leads us over temptation.

In light of that, there are practical ways in which God teaches us to say no to sin and to say yes to Him. But the source is Christ. He is our strength. He is our wisdom. He is our power. He is our life. That's why Colossians 2:6 tells us that we are to live our lives in Christ the same way we received Him—by faith.

Many people think the Christian life is a passive life that involves no effort or participation on our end. But that's not the truth. Yes, we are saved and forgiven and accepted by grace alone and not by our effort or works. But the mystery of our union with Christ is that He lives His life through us and we also live. Paul said, "I labor, striving according to His power" (Colossians 1:29), and in 1 Corinthians 15:10, he said, "I labored even more than all of them, yet not I, but the grace of God with me."

Our strength and our source and our energy all come from Him. Throughout this book, when I speak of dependence and trust, I'm not saying we're lifeless puppets. We're involved, and God is living in us and through us.

Hearing from God

In order to learn from Jesus, we need to understand what His voice is like. One litmus test is this: if what you're hearing isn't setting you free, then it's not from Jesus. He said, "And you will know the truth, and the truth will set you free" (John 8:32). Another could be: if it's not bringing you rest, then it's not from Jesus. Remember, He promised rest for our souls (see Matthew 11:29). Furthermore, if it contradicts what we find in Scripture, then we need to question it. God has spoken to us by His Son (Hebrews 1:2) and has inspired the Scriptures to teach us (2 Timothy 3:16). Jesus promised that we would hear His voice (John 10:27). But His voice will never contradict what Scripture has clearly revealed to us.

The Enemy lies to us, and thoughts about our past creep into our minds. If you're like me, you've given them too much of a voice, and after a while you start actually believing what they say. These thoughts are enemies of your mind, seeking to "steal, kill, and destroy" (John 10:10). The Enemy wants to steal your joy; Jesus wants to be your joy. The Enemy wants to kill your happiness; Jesus wants to be your happiness. The Enemy wants to destroy peace; the Prince of Peace wants to give you a peace that surpasses understanding. The Enemy is your accuser; Jesus is your Advocate. The Enemy condemns you; Jesus comforts you.

I don't hear audibly from Jesus. Most Christians I know don't either. But through the inspiration of the Spirit inside us, the Bible, and others, God speaks. God is not a God of confusion but of peace (1 Corinthians 14:33). So as you filter the thoughts, beliefs, and messages in your mind, remember that whatever is not bringing you peace, freedom, rest, and joy is not from God!

Bank tellers will tell you that the best way to recognize counterfeit currency isn't to study a bunch of counterfeit bills, but to spend time with the real bills. The best way to recognize the truth of God's voice versus the lies we hear is to continue to spend time immersed in His truth.

Teaching Us in Temptation

Jesus was tempted in all ways in order to help us in all our temptations (Hebrews 4:15). Just because you are tempted, doesn't mean you're doing something wrong. Temptation is not sin. The good news is that Jesus always gives us a way out of temptation (1 Corinthians 10:13). As we look at how Jesus teaches us and how He gives us practical ways to deal with temptation, realize that these are not simple formulas that you can just plug into your life and *bam*, you start living sin-free.

I still struggle every single day, but what I've discovered is that when I actually believe, know, and practice what Scripture teaches me, over time I see the fruit. Scripture gives us a plan, not a secret formula, to face temptation and sin.

In temptation, Jesus is inviting us to look to Him. Second Timothy 2:22 says we can flee from sin. Maybe that happens through remembering a promise He's made us in His Word, or maybe it is choosing to think about something else. For example, in the Gospel of Luke, we see Jesus being tempted by the Enemy, and Jesus used God's Word to combat the temptations.

Hebrews 12:1 tells us to focus on Jesus in order to lay aside the sin that trips us up. And Paul tells us in Colossians 3:1 and Philippians 4:8 to set our minds on things above and to think on things that are worthy of praise. So, as we turn our attention to Jesus, we naturally turn away from whatever is tempting us in the moment.

In our temptations, Jesus is not far off. He's right there with us, empowering us to say no to sin. He always gives us a way out. It's important for you to know that you are dead to the power of sin (Romans 6:11). This means sin cannot control you. You actually want what Jesus wants. You don't want to sin. Romans 6:18 says you crave doing what is right. You're a slave to it. I know it doesn't feel that way—we're all still learning that—but it's the truth. In our struggle with sin, we need to believe that we don't want it. We have the power to not choose sin by God's Spirit in us.

The apostle Paul is practical on this too. He says if you have a stealing problem, work with your hands (Ephesians 4:28). If you struggle with gossip, slander, or any unwholesome talk, then encourage and build others up instead (Ephesians 4:28–29). Perhaps you struggle with pride. Paul would probably say, "You are who you are by the grace of God," so be obsessed with Jesus and His accomplishments, not your own.

Saturate your mind with the goodness and truth of God. Research shows us that those who engage four times a week with the truth of God's Word are 59 percent less likely to view porn, 30 percent less likely to struggle with loneliness, and more prone to say no to sin.[43]

I love that Hebrews 12:1–2 tells us to simply look to Jesus in order to live free from the sin that entangles us. The author of Hebrews doesn't tell us to try harder or do more or exert more effort. The answer is to look to Jesus—the One who gives us faith, sustains us, empowers us, and "is able to keep you from stumbling, and to make you stand in the presence of His glory blameless with great joy" (Jude 24).

"I need to work on sinning less," we say as we try harder to say no to sin. Yet that's not the method God wants us to take. He wants us to fix our thoughts on Jesus. The work isn't to "sin less." Instead, we're told to trust Jesus. And as we trust Jesus, we will naturally sin less.

In your struggle with lust, whether it is fantasy or porn, you need to know that Jesus loves you through it. If you're addicted, get help! Reach out to a pastor, friend, or counselor. You're not alone in your struggle. It's a struggle that both men and women deal with. On a practical level, you can adjust the settings on your phone and computer and you can disable anything that is inappropriate on your TV. Then clear out any clutter or tempting thing on your social media feed. Don't follow people who post explicit things.

You're dead to sin and you're alive to God (Romans 6:11). You're not a lustful person. You're a child of God who struggles with lust. That is why each time you choose sin, you're miserable. That proves that you're a new creation. The truth is that you're no longer a slave to sin; you're now obedient to God from your heart (Romans 6:17).

There are many decisions we make leading up to sin. We don't just accidently stumble upon porn or accidently gossip, and we don't randomly steal or blow up at someone. Christ in us is empowering us to choose to say no. We may have to say a lot of nos. It's not like we can say no once and expect the temptation to immediately disappear.

I'll say it again: the most important thing to understand is that you're not alone in this. You have Christ in you, empowering you to say no to sin. The beauty of your new heart is that you want to say no to sin too. God isn't asking you to do something that you don't want to do. Since God has killed your old self and given you a new self, you no longer want to sin (Romans 6:5–11).

There's a great illustration about Christ in us that I heard a preacher make recently. He took a glove and placed it on his Bible. He then said that this glove was remarkable and special—because it could actually pick up the Bible. The pastor said, "Glove, pick up the Bible." Nothing happened. He said it again: "Glove, pick up the Bible." Again, nothing. The third time, he slipped his hand inside the glove and said, "Glove, pick up the Bible." You know what happened? The glove lifted the Bible off the table.

This may seem like a silly illustration, but it makes a great point about Christ living His life through us. Christ in us enables us to say no to sin. It's not about our ability to imitate Jesus or use the WWJD approach. Instead, we can trust in the strengthening power of Christ living His life in us. We still have to make a choice. We have to choose whether or not to let Christ live His life through us. This isn't a "let go, let God" approach. It's our living by Christ's power in our temptation. As we trust Christ and His strength in every moment, then we start choosing His ways.

Whatever your struggle may be, whether lust, pride, anger, lying, or something else, that's not who you are. You're a child of God who is righteous and holy. You're not what you do, what you've done, or what you will do. You are who God says you are. Your struggle is with sin, but you are not sin. Jesus is teaching us, through temptations, that we are not what we think or do, and that the path He has for us is more fulfilling than anything sin has to offer.

Teaching us Each Day

Each day, Jesus's goal is to show us how loved we are. In every moment, He's teaching us about who He is, who we are, and how to live our lives rooted and grounded in His love for us. Further, He's teaching us to focus on His finished work, not our sins. God wants us focused on His Son, not our past failures. He wants us to recognize that we are one spirit with Christ. This means there are no obstacles or hindrances between us and Christ. Nothing can separate us. He wants us to learn who we are in Him, that we're complete, righteous, holy, accepted, and flawless in Him.

Jesus primarily teaches us through His written Word (the Bible) and through community. He wants us to learn from each other, and He wants to use us to minister to others. He also wants to encourage and equip and build us up through others—whether that is at a Sunday service, a small group during the week, or over coffee with friends. I encourage you to get involved with other believers.

We're not called to merely look back and do what Jesus did in the Gospels. Instead, we're called to look within to the risen Christ and let Him live through us. The Teacher is in us, inspiring our every move: "In Him we move and live and have our being" (Acts 17:28).

CHAPTER 14

He Assures

"Therefore there is now no condemnation at all
for those who are in Christ Jesus."

Romans 8:1

A survey done recently by Baylor University found that around 150 million Americans believe in an angry God.[44] With this in mind, it's no wonder that when we sin, we don't go to God but instead try to move away from Him. When we sin, we often feel separated from God, scared of Him, or just embarrassed.

We think God is reacting to our sin with disgust, anger, or at least disappointment. I used to think that way too, until I read about the life of Jesus. In the last chapter of this book, we looked at how Jesus teaches us in temptation, but what does He do when we sin?

I don't know how many times I (as a child) packed up a few toys and some clothes, and found a stick to hold the pouch of things I'd gathered because I was running away. Sometimes I even made it past the pond on our land before I got hungry. My response to getting in trouble or having a disagreement with my parents was to run away. And I used to think the same way when it came to Jesus. Just like when I was a kid, I didn't realize I was running away from everything I needed.

I used to believe that when I sinned, I needed to run away from Jesus because He was mad at me. I now know that when I sin, I need to talk to Him because He loves me and is for me. I'm not scared of going to Him anymore. Many people think they have the ability to run from God. That can't even happen. We're in Christ forever (Romans 8:9), so when we sin or try to run from God, He goes with us, no matter what.

Jesus is not your accuser. The Enemy is your accuser. We need to know the difference. Next time you sin, if the voice you hear is accusing, condemning, shaming, or guilting you, it isn't the voice of Jesus. Jesus is in the business of assuring us in the midst of accusation. He comforts us when we're feeling condemned, silencing our shame and giving us abundant grace for our guilt.

Of course, the Holy Spirit teaches us and corrects us, but He never does it with shame, guilt, or condemnation. He's our Counselor and Comforter, not our accuser and condemner. Hebrews 10:15–17 tells us that the Holy Spirit is testifying to us that God remembers our sins no more! He doesn't want us to focus on our sin, and He doesn't hurl guilt our way because of our sin. Instead, He reminds us of the finished work and of who we are in Christ and how to live free from sin.

Jesus didn't ask the thief on the cross to justify his wrongdoing. He didn't seek an apology or tears. The thief asked Jesus to remember him, and what did Jesus do? Did He shame Him for his sins? Did He give him a long lecture on how he was wicked and bad? No. Jesus just said, "Today you will be with me in paradise." You don't clean yourself up before you come to Jesus. You go to Jesus and He makes you clean.

This is the "glorious gospel of the blessed God" that Paul was entrusted to preach (1 Timothy 1:11). The word *blessed* in that verse can also be translated "happy." Our God is happy. He wants none to perish. He *so* loves you and me, and it's His relentless passion to convince us that we can trust Him in every moment.

One of Jesus's best friends, Peter, denied him three times when Jesus needed him most. Peter claimed he didn't know Jesus because he was scared of being associated with Him, but after the resurrection, Jesus didn't shame Peter or condemn him, or even question his friendship or faith (Jesus had even predicted it would happen). Instead, He told Peter that he would be one of the leaders of the church, essentially assuring him that his sin didn't disqualify him from being used by God.

You might say, "Yes, Zach, but you don't understand. My sins are big!" Well, have you heard about the apostle Paul? Before he met Jesus, he was standing by, giving approval to kill Christians. Yes, murder. And he said he was the worst sinner he knew (1 Timothy 1:15). Yet, what happened when He met Jesus? He got transformed. Jesus actually called him a "chosen instrument" (Acts 9:15). Your past, your current mistakes, your struggle with sin—these cannot separate you from Jesus's love or disqualify you from being used by Him.

To say that your sin is "too big" for God is to say that the cross is "too little" for your sin. The cross is greater than any sin you will ever commit. You cannot out-sin the grace of God (Romans 5:20). The cross is enough for you, in every single moment. It worked. It is finished. God will never get tired of bearing your burdens and sustaining you with His grace. He never said, "I'll save you and get you started, but then you'll need to take it from there." No, God promises that He will finish what He started in you (Philippians 1:6).

Now don't misunderstand me. There are physical, earthly consequences for your sin. If you steal and get caught, you may get fined or go to jail. If you cheat on a test, you may fail it. If you lie about work, you may get fired. But the spiritual consequences—separation from God, anger, or disappointment—have been taken care of through the cross and resurrection. That's the good news of what Christ has done for us.

Yes, we can grieve the Spirit, but just like a mother who grieves when her child disobeys and runs out into the street, Jesus grieves when we choose sin. He isn't mad; He just wants what's best for us. There's a big difference. The consequence for our sin is death. Anything less minimizes the seriousness of sin, but Jesus became our sin and died for us so we would never have to deal with the spiritual consequence of sin (Romans 6:23).

First John 2 tells us that when we sin, we have Jesus as our advocate. It doesn't say that when we sin, we lose our salvation or lose God's love or lose fellowship with God or that God is going to punish us. We think when we sin, we have to get God to like us again. But that isn't the truth. The glorious truth of the New Covenant is that Christ is in us, His face is always toward us, and He will never, ever forsake us! In 1 John 2, after John says, "When we sin," he doesn't give us ten things we need to do. Instead, he tells us what Jesus is *already* doing for us.

Jesus as our advocate doesn't mean what most think. It's not that Jesus and God the Father are arguing against each other. God the Father isn't against us. Jesus isn't convincing God the Father to love us or forgive us. Instead, Jesus, the one who dealt with our sins forever, is seated by the Father as proof to *us* that His work is effective and enough. He is our advocate, He is our forgiveness, and He is our righteousness (1 Corinthians 1:30). It's only in Him that we are forgiven and righteous, and can stand blameless in God's presence (1 Corinthians 1:8).

So when we sin, we don't have to fear because there will never be a moment when God the Father isn't reminded that what Jesus did was enough and effective. And when we sin, we don't have to make our case or beg or plead for God to forgive us again. Our advocate is Jesus, the One who has finished His work once and for all. Remember, He is seated because His work is done (Hebrews 10:12).

I understand that this sounds scary to many, but fear and shame will never produce love or devotion to God. So it's time we stop using that tactic to get believers to "shape up." What we need most in the midst of our own shame and regret and guilt is a big dose of God's grace and love.

Jesus does a number of things when we sin. He constantly dispels any doubts we have of His love, His forgiveness, and His care for us. I'm not saying God approves of our sin. I'm saying Jesus assures us of His work, His love, and His grace for us when and after we sin. We need to know that God isn't caught off guard or surprised when we sin. We're not "letting God down" or "disappointing" Him. Why? He saw it coming. And He took our disappointing moments away, forever. His deepest desire is to meet our sins and failures with His grace every single time (Romans 5:20).

Remember yearbook day in school? It was the day, usually during the last week of the school year, when you would get your yearbook and then have it signed by your friends. Most of the time you'd just get a signature, but sometimes you'd get encouraging words from someone, maybe even unexpectedly. Those few special notes would keep you on cloud nine for the entire summer.

God's given us His note to us through His Word. It's not filled with a list of to-dos or a laundry list of our sins. Instead, we discover His promises and His outrageous love and grace to us.

Romans 8:38–39 gives us an unshakeable confidence in God's love by declaring that nothing—not even ourselves—can separate us from His unfailing, limitless love. John 10:28 shouts to us that nothing can snatch us from God's hand. Romans 15:7 tells us that nothing can alter God's acceptance of us. And Hebrews 7:25 says we're saved forever because Jesus always lives to intercede for us.

Romans 8:1 is a verse that could revolutionize your relationship with Jesus. You might want to have it tattooed or maybe printed on a T-shirt. It says there's no condemnation for you and me. No punishment. No lightning bolt. No disgust. Nothing. That is why the New Testament tells us that we are blameless (Jude 24; Colossians 1:22; 1 Corinthians 1:8). We have peace with God (Romans 5:1). He's not mad at us! And He's not ashamed to call us His own (Hebrews 2:11; 11:16).

God is calling us to root our lives in His promises to us. We have this hope as an anchor for the soul, firm and secure (Hebrews 6:19). This hope is Jesus. If He says it, then we can trust it. So what if, the next time you sin, you go boldly to the throne of grace (Hebrews 4:16)? It's a throne of grace, not a throne of shame. And Hebrews 4:16 tells us that we can enter it with confidence, not fear.

At the cross, Jesus experienced all of the shame from your sin. The last thing He wants is for you to experience it too. It's not yours to carry. Your failures don't mean grace doesn't work. Shame tries to convince us that we should hide, and that God's forgiveness isn't that big. Shame tells us that God is mad. But grace is inviting us to trust in the God who is not defined by our shame. Grace is inviting us to believe the God of all grace—who gave Himself for us because He loves us. Shame wants to convince us that we must perform or work for or earn God's acceptance and love each time we sin. But the good news of the cross and resurrection is that we are loved and accepted and enough—in every single moment.

Jesus doesn't want you to hide. Shame calls out your sin; Jesus calls out your name. You're His. You're hidden with Christ in God (Colossians 3:3). This means you're safe and secure in the warm embrace of God. Jesus will finish what He started in you (Philippians 1:6). You can be assured that you're totally forgiven, unconditionally loved, and forever accepted, no matter what. God does not lie (Titus 1:2). His promises are unshakeable and unbreakable because they rest on His faithfulness to you, not on your faithfulness or obedience to Him. "If we are faithless, He remains faithful" (2 Timothy 2:13).

You can't diminish the love God has for you. This is why the New Testament tells us that we are already citizens of heaven (Philippians 3:20). And this is why Peter tells us that we have an "inheritance which is imperishable, undefiled, and will not fade away, reserved in heaven for you" (1 Peter 1:4). Once we understand that we are secure, it doesn't make us want to take advantage of it. Instead, it enables us to trust Jesus in our darkest moments. Every time you make a bad choice, God goes with you and He stays with you. He's committed to you, to your growth, and to conforming you to the image of His Son (Romans 8:29).

We love to imagine a really "big sin" that could break the deal. Jesus responds with "I remember their sins no more" (Hebrews 10:17, my paraphrase) and "the one who comes to Me I will certainly not cast out" (John 6:37).

First John 5:13 says that we can know that we have eternal life. And God's goal for us is to convince us that we are saved—no matter what. This is why He gave us the Holy Spirit and sealed us with Him (Ephesians 1:13). We can't lose the Spirit, therefore we can't lose our salvation. It wasn't our lack of sinning that saved us. Therefore, it can't be our continued sinning that "unsaves" us. Scripture says we are born again. We cannot become unborn.

Our salvation is Jesus's work from start to finish, and He promises "to keep you from stumbling, and to present you blameless before the presence of his glory with great joy" (Jude 24 ESV).

Is This a License to Sin?

When I thought I could lose my salvation and status with Jesus, it caused me to sin more, not less. When I thought Jesus was mad at me and never pleased with me, it caused me to rebel against God, not love Him. It's been over eight years since I discovered the truth about God's grace and His new covenant way of grace. This discovery is the reason I've devoted my entire life to sharing the gospel with the world.

I discovered relationship with Jesus, not religion. I fell in love with Him. God's love will never lead us to sin more. Never. Just like with my wife, whose unconditional love for me doesn't make me want to take advantage of it and run off and cheat on her. Instead, her love makes me want to love her more! God's love compels us to love, not sin (2 Corinthians 5:14).

Paul knew that after He said, "Where sin increased, grace abounded" (Romans 5:20 ESV), it would scare some people. That's why, in Romans 6, he explained why grace doesn't lead us *to* sin, but *from* sin. In that chapter, Paul said the believer is "united with [Christ]" (6:5 ESV), "set free from sin" (6:7 ESV), "dead to sin and alive to God" (6:11 ESV), "instruments for righteousness" (6:12 ESV), and "obedient from the heart" (6:17 ESV). This shatters the idea that "too much grace" is a "license to sin."

Our motivation to avoid sin is rooted in the new identity God has given us. Sure, we cannot out-sin God's grace (Romans 5:20), but by God's grace, we no longer want to! We don't want to sin since we are now slaves of righteousness (Romans 6:18). Yes, we all stumble in many ways (James 3:2), but as children of God, we now want what God wants. The apostle Paul gives us plenty of reasons to avoid sin and not abuse grace, but he never motivates us by threatening our salvation or telling us we need more forgiveness or claiming that God will leave us. We avoid sin because it doesn't fulfill us and our heart longs to walk in newness of life.

Understanding God's grace empowers us to sin no more. It teaches us to say no to sin by giving us the freedom to discover that we really want what God wants. We are new creations! The old you was crucified (Romans 6:5; Galatians 2:20). You're a new person, a partaker of the divine nature, and you have the power of Christ living in you and through you to do what pleases God (2 Corinthians 5:17; 2 Peter 1:3; Philippians 2:13).

PART 4:

BETTER THAN SELF-HELP

"God had provided something better for us."

Hebrews 11:40

"For You have been a stronghold for the helpless."

Isaiah 25:4

CHAPTER 15

He's Our Comforter

"Blessed be the God and Father of our Lord Jesus Christ, the Father of
mercies and God of all comfort, who comforts us in all our affliction."
2 Corinthians 1:3–4

Intense agony. Overwhelmed with sorrow to the point He felt like dying, His sweat became like drops of blood. This rare condition, known as hematohidrosis, occurs because of intense anxiety and agony. This is what Jesus experienced the night before He would go to the cross *for you.* Hebrews 12:2 says it was "for the joy set before Him" that He endured all the pain and suffering of the cross. That joy was the possibility of relationship with you.

When you are suffering, you don't need a self-help message. "Just do it," "optimize," "do this and your life will be full," "figure it out," "work harder," "accomplish more," and "enough is never enough" don't cut it. What's saddening is, the messages heard in many churches are similar: "love more," "try harder," "obey more and your life will be full," "have more faith," "be strong and courageous." Or my favorite, "God helps those who help themselves."

Self-help is a lot like learning to wakeboard for the first time. You think that in order to stand up and start wakeboarding, it's up to you to pull yourself up and get going. But the moment the boat starts and you try to pull yourself up is the moment you go face first in the lake and get a mouthful of water. Isn't this like life? You try so hard to make it all work, but you end up on your face.

The trick to wakeboarding is to let the boat pull you up. It's about trusting the boat to do its work. It's not about striving to pull yourself up. The same is true with the Christian life. We live by trusting Christ, not by our own effort.

We often think it's our job to get ourselves out of our pain and suffering. We think Jesus is on the other side of our sorrow and that with enough faith, effort, or obedience, we will "break through." What if God is not on the other side of our mess, but inside our mess comforting us? We have made God into a self-help guru who will help only those who are strong and obedient and worthy of His attention. The Christian life isn't about striving for God; it's about trusting God. It's not about pulling ourselves up; it's about letting God comfort us and keep us standing.

We look in the mirror, or at our car, our house, our accomplishments, or our Instagram feed, and the lie we believe is, *I'm not enough.* "Don't give up," we're told. Keep pushing through. We're constantly searching and seeking to be enough, and nothing ever seems to satisfy or work. Perhaps this is why two-thirds of people under thirty-five don't feel cared for.[45] We need to know that Jesus deeply cares for us. That He's not asking us to do this on our own, but instead to look to Him. And He's placed people in our lives who care for us. Ditch the lie that says people or God don't care for you.

The good news of Jesus is that in Him, you're enough. You're no longer defined by your failures or successes. We can give up and actually give in to who Jesus is. That's called dependency. We don't have to push through; the work for our acceptance and worth is finished.

The message of the cross is "It is finished." We live our entire lives under Jesus's declaration of "Done." All the work that needed to be done to make us right and accepted by God has been accomplished by Jesus. We don't need to do more, we don't need to make our life count, and we don't need to prove ourselves or obey more or be strong or do anything to be more right with God.

The cross and resurrection prove that Jesus's love and care for us happens independent of what we do for Him. When we go to Jesus, we go to someone who actually understands us. Every emotion. Every feeling. Every pain. Every darkest moment and wondering and suffering and difficult circumstance and broken relationship and regret of sin. He gets us because He was tempted in all ways and can sympathize with what we go through (Hebrews 4:15).

Jesus was sad to the point of weeping because of His friend's death (John 11:35). He took naps because of His exhaustion (Mark 4:38). He grew weary in Samaria (John 4:6). He was disturbed and angry and even grew hungry (Matthew 4:2; Mark 6:6; John 2:15). He endured all of these emotions because He knew you would eventually feel them. He knew that you would face pain, so He came to not only face it but make it possible that one day He could take away your pain forever. Jesus never shames us for our needs but responds "generously and without reproach" (James 1:5). We're not supposed to live strong. Jesus invites us to live weak and trust Him for everything (2 Corinthians 12:9).

Jesus is the "God of all comfort" (2 Corinthians 1:3). There will never be a moment when He isn't comforting you. Jesus is committed to caring for and protecting those who are His children, which means we can actually ask Him for help because He doesn't help those who can help themselves. He helps only those who *cannot* help themselves (and that's all of us). You can cast "all your anxiety on him." Why? "Because he cares for you" (1 Peter 5:7). Since Jesus is in charge of our needs, we can give Him everything that bothers us.

Earlier, I mentioned that when I was a youth pastor, I was burned out and felt like I was barely hanging on to Jesus. After one Wednesday night youth service, I was driving home and felt like giving up on everything. I thought, *If I disappear, will anyone notice or care?* It was perhaps the lowest point of my life. Life didn't seem worth living. I'd lost all hope, and it felt like nothing I did mattered. It felt like *I* didn't matter.

I don't know about you, but I can be real good at faking it. Not only with others, but with God. Crazy, right? I stopped talking to God about my problems because I didn't want to be needy. I knew that He was enough, but I didn't really believe it. That night on the way home, I started opening up to God, telling Him my frustrations and needs and concerns and how He wasn't enough for me. Looking back, that was one of the most freeing things I've ever done. By God's grace, He showed me the people in my life who cared for me and used them to bring great comfort.

The most important thing He showed me is that the Christian life is not about working hard to hang on to Jesus. The Christian life is based on the promise that Jesus is always holding on to us, no matter how faithless and weak we are. It's okay to have needs. God designed us that way. He designed us to need Him. And He revealed to me that He truly is enough for me even if I don't feel like He is.

As our comforter, Jesus wants us to come to Him and pray to Him. I used to think prayer was about getting something from God, but now I know that prayer is talking with the One who's already given me everything I need in Him.

Talking with God

Sometimes, I'm not very good at communicating with God. Prayer can feel weird, pointless, and difficult. But prayer—or simply, talking with God—allows us to speak directly to our great Comforter. God loves to hear you! He wants to know your needs. The promise of Philippians 4:19 is, "My God will meet all your needs according to the riches of his glory in Christ Jesus" (NIV).

Talking with Jesus about my day, my needs, my worries, and my struggles has become one of my favorite things to do. I've never heard God's voice audibly, but I know He's listening and I know that through His people and through His written Word and through His Spirit in me, He's speaking. I don't pray because I believe prayer has some special "power." I pray because God is powerful. I don't believe in the power of prayer; I believe in the power of God, which is the only reason I pray. Prayer isn't some secret formula we use to get something from God.

He's not a genie or a slot machine. He's our Father, our Friend, and our Comforter. Prayer isn't an emotional feeling. More times than not, you'll feel nothing when you talk with God. That's normal. I don't have a formula in place when I talk to my friends. I just talk. I'm real. I'm honest. So you can throw out the King James English and the acronyms, and just have a conversation. Prayer is talking with your heavenly Father. It can involve asking, thanking, adoring, confessing, or just talking about your day. There's not a right way or a wrong way to pray.

Perhaps the most important thing to know is that prayer *isn't* about getting closer to God. Scripture is clear: We are one spirit with God (1 Corinthians 6:17), brought near to God by Christ's blood (Ephesians 2:13), and hidden with Christ (Colossians 3:3), and Christ is living in our hearts (Ephesians 3:17). How much closer can you get than hidden, indwelt, and one Spirit? He's in you, forever! Sure, we learn more about Jesus, but we're not getting closer to God through our prayer and devotion.

When you pray, God's attention is yours, all the time. He's cleared out His entire schedule just to be with you. His face and His eyes are always on you (1 Peter 3:12). We're not talking to "the man upstairs" or a God far off in heaven. He's *in* you!

Prayer allows us to give our cares to God, to give thanks, and to seek wisdom. And prayer ultimately helps us to see our desperate need for God in every moment. As we begin learning more and more about the love and grace of God, prayer allows us to be open and real with our great Comforter and for us to lean into Him.

Jesus prayed for you (John 17:20–25). He prayed that you would be one with Him and the Father. He still prays for you (Romans 8:26). Even when you don't know what to say, the Spirit intercedes on your behalf. That's good news. There's no pressure on you to muster up the right words.

So ask Jesus for help. When you're worried, stressed, or anxious, let that be a trigger to let Him carry your load. He cares deeply for you, so cast your cares on Him. You don't have to hide or be afraid; your God is for you (Romans 8:31), not against you. And nothing delights Him more than when His child climbs up in His lap and shares with Him.

Our Shepherd

Jesus describes His work in our lives through the image of a shepherd. "I am the good shepherd" (John 10:11, 14), Jesus says. This means that everything we need, we already have in Christ. Jesus is our source for life. He is the One who leads us and guides us and cares for us. Since everything we need we have in Him, we don't need anything else. We don't have to search for comfort or hope or peace anywhere else because we have it in Christ. Second Peter 1:3 tells us, "His divine power has granted to us everything pertaining to life and godliness." Colossians 2:10 tells us that we have been "made complete." Our great Shepherd has rigged it to where we lack nothing. We don't need more!

So what does this look like? Are we supposed to muster enough faith to "appropriate this" or access it? Not quite. Often, we place too much emphasis on willpower or having more faith. But anytime the message takes our attention off Christ, we need to be careful. It's not the strength or power of our faith that does anything; it's the Object of our faith that makes the difference.

God has given us each a measure of faith (Romans 12:3). This means faith is a gift from God that comes by hearing the Word of Christ (Romans 10:17). So no matter what we feel in a given moment, we're not lacking. And we don't need "more faith."

The Christian life is not rooted and anchored in our devotion and commitment to God, but in God's devotion and commitment to us. The Christian life is not based on our determination and willpower. It's not "do your part and then God will do His." No, the Christian life is God's work from start to finish. We're fully dependent upon Christ for everything. He's the source, He's our strength, and He's working in us and through us.

He's Really This Good

Jesus is really this good. I know many of you may be thinking, *There's no way God is this good.* But He is. It's not that God doesn't care when we sin or doesn't care about our behavior. He does! But remember, He dealt with our sin at the cross. And it worked!

God cares deeply about our behavior, but He's not punishing us when we mess up. The punishment was death, and Jesus already died. God is unlike any teacher or trainer we've ever had. He's able to train us and comfort us and teach us without ever using shame or guilt. We need to clear the clutter and realize that God is love and everything He does is loving. He's for us, not against us.

God is working all things for your good (Romans 8:28). He is not the cause of all things, but He does cause all things to work for your good. He's not the creator of your bad circumstances; He's your Comforter in the midst of your bad circumstances.

CHAPTER 16

He's Our Renewer

"Our inner person is being renewed day by day."
2 Corinthians 4:16

Scars from our past. Guilt over sin. Labels that we still wear. A shame-based identity. Many of us feel broken, hurt, and in pain, and don't know where to find lasting healing. The message of self-help is that we are in charge of our own healing. The pressure is on us to do more, optimize our life, and strive for a standard we can never meet.

You're not alone in your hurt and pain. And you don't need to be ashamed of the things that have brought you hurt or pain. Jesus's goal is to heal us, not hurt us. We need to recognize that Jesus is for us and longs for us to start believing truth that will set us free. The promise of Scripture is that we can be "transformed by the renewing of [our] mind" (Romans 12:2).

How would you describe your physical appearance?

In 2013, the personal care brand Dove made a short film called *Real Beauty Sketches*. In it, they explored the gap between how others perceive us and how we perceive ourselves. They had an FBI-trained forensic artist draw two portraits. One was based on the woman's own description of herself and the other based on a stranger's description.

The results were pretty surprising. The portraits drawn from the stranger's description were always more beautiful than the ones drawn from the woman's own description. So often, because of past labels, shame, and hurt, we don't see ourselves as we are. And women and men alike don't see themselves as beautiful and as handsome as they are.

We've done the same thing spiritually. We don't see ourselves the way God does. But thankfully we don't have to wonder what God thinks of us. He says, "Masterpiece" (Ephesians 2:10 NLT).

I love the story about Jesus healing a leper. The leper came to Him and said, "If You are willing, You can make me clean" (Matthew 8:2). Many of us wonder if God cares about us—if He knows our needs and cares to do anything about our past, our shame, and our pain. Jesus answered the man, "I am willing; be cleansed" (v. 3). *I am willing*. Jesus is not withholding Himself from us. He's given us Himself, forever. And now He is in us, renewing us and leading us to truth that sets us free.

"Four eyes," "Fatso," "Stupid"—whatever the nickname, it hurts and usually it sticks. Mine was "Four eyes." The worst thing about being called a name is that it usually refers to something you can't help. I couldn't fix my eyes. The words hurt. It is also true that, if believed for too long, some hurtful words ("you're not enough," "you're not pretty," "you're not man enough," "you don't have what it takes," "you'll never be wanted") become beliefs. Eventually, those mean words sound like they're coming from ourselves.

I was the fastest kid in my elementary school. My nickname was "Rabbit" because of my speed. I loved that name! It affirmed me and the talent I had. Do you see the power a name has? The power one nickname or label can give someone? It can either build them up or tear them down. This is why God is renewing us day by day (2 Corinthians 4:16). And this is why God wants us to renew our minds each day (Romans 12:2).

The fastest man to ever live has the last name of Bolt. There's actually a hypothesis called nominative determinism that says people tend to gravitate toward a profession that fits their name, and there's a lot of proof that seems to back this hypothesis up. A baseball player with the last name Fielder or a weather reporter named Storm or a chiropractor named McCracken seem to lend some credibility. I'm not making this up! Fortunately, or unfortunately, we often live out the names and labels we carry.

At my in-laws' house, whenever there's a birthday, the birthday boy/girl gets a special red plate that says "You are special." The first time they celebrated my birthday, not only did I get the plate, but each person went around and said something nice and encouraging about me. They call this getting showered. Words have power. And the things we say about ourselves and the encouragement we get from others can actually catapult us into believing who we really are as God's children.

Up to this point, we've talked about our identity in Christ only briefly. But we need to know that in Christ, nothing is wrong with us. Through the cross, you were crucified (Romans 6:5; Galatians 2:20), you were buried (Romans 6:6), and you were brought to life as a new creation! This means your struggle is no longer against yourself because there is only one you—the new creation God has made.

Our struggle is not against a "sinful nature" inside of us. That was crucified with Christ and buried! That phrase isn't even in most translations of the Bible. The word best used is *flesh*, which is simply your old way of thinking and living.[46] Our struggle is with the Enemy, the power of sin, and our old habits, our old thoughts, and the labels we still wear. The thoughts that we get each day aren't coming from some bad part of us; they are coming from outside of us (sin and the accuser). That's why God is leading us to renew our minds and take every thought captive.

We're not sinful by nature. Our new spirit is not a sinful one. Instead, Scripture says we are "partakers of the divine nature" (2 Peter 1:4). We're not sinful, we're saints. What God says about us is true. He doesn't lie. What He says, He means. It's reality. God wouldn't call us saints if we were really dirty sinners. He says we're saints because that's who He's made us to be.

Shame has convinced us that we can't change—that we are defined by our failures, mistakes, and behavior. But at the moment of salvation, we were changed. Actually, an exchange happened. Jesus took our old self and gave us a new one. And then He infused us with His life. Now we are spending the rest of our life maturing into who God has already made us. As we learn who we are in Christ, our thoughts and behavior and habits start being transformed.

One lie about our identity is that we are what we do. This is why so many Christians are running around calling themselves "sinners." We believe that we are defined by our sins. But according to Scripture, we did nothing to become sinners. That's right, the apostle Paul says we're all born in Adam and therefore all sinners (Romans 5:19)). In the same way, we do nothing for us to become righteous or to get in Christ. We were *reborn* that way. This is what it means to be born again.

First John 5:1 says we are "born of God." God is not a dirty, rotten sinner. That's not who He is. Since we're now in His family and carry His name, we're defined by Him. Our name comes from Him. We're a child of God. And as a child of God, our name is *saint, beloved, righteous, holy, blameless*.

There was a great exchange that happened at the cross. Jesus took our sin and gave us His righteousness. Jesus didn't commit any sins and yet became sin. And we did nothing—no righteous works—and yet we have become the righteousness of God (2 Corinthians 5:21).[47] We became sinners through Adam's disobedience, and we became righteous from Jesus's obedience (Romans 5:19). This means we get our identity from who we are *in*. Believers are always in Christ and in the Spirit (Romans 8:9). We have been transferred into the kingdom of God's beloved Son (Colossians 1:13).

Many people claim that God "sees us this way" only because our identity is "heavenly." However, did Jesus really take your sin or was that fake? Furthermore, did God only "see you" as sinful before Christ? Of course not! In the same way, God sees you as righteous because He's made you righteous by uniting you with Christ! This is real, not just positional or heavenly. God says you are His masterpiece. I've never heard a painter say they can't stand to look at a masterpiece or that they'd rather have another painting cover up a masterpiece.

In 2017, the *Salvator Mundi*, a six-hundred-year-old painting by Leonardo da Vinci, sold for $450 million. It's a masterpiece. It was the most expensive painting ever sold at auction. No matter where that painting is placed—a museum, in a shack in Montana, a subway station—it doesn't change its value.

The same is true of you. No matter what you've done, where you are in life, or what circumstances you find yourself in, you cannot lose your value. You cannot lose your worth. God loves what He sees when He looks at you.

First Peter 3:12 assures us that the "eyes of the Lord are toward the righteous." The Hebrew word for *presence* can also be translated as "face." When Adam and Eve sinned, they hid from God's presence (or face). Many today teach that God is hiding His face from us. But remember, it was God who sought out Adam and Eve in the garden after they sinned. God is not hiding His face from you. God loves what He sees when He looks at you!

In the New Testament, the word *sinner* never refers to a believer. Sinners are called ungodly (Jude 1:15) and are separated from Christ (Hebrews 7:26). When you do a search for the word *saint* in the New Testament, you see the word used more than sixty times, and it's always referring to those who believe in Christ. It's not just for Saint Nick or Mother Teresa. The Corinthian church was one of the craziest churches in the New Testament. They acted in ways that were completely ungodly, yet Paul called them saints (1 Corinthians 1:2; 2:1).

In Paul's letters to the Romans, Ephesians, Philippians, and Colossians, he opens by calling the people in these churches *saints*. He never says, "To the sinners saved by grace" or "To the wretched children of God." Nope, *saints* is our new name. That's who we are. *Saint* is not a term for those who are morally better than others. It's for those who believe in Jesus Christ. We're God's holy ones, His saints, and it is a result of God's work, not our performance.

We are not sinners any longer. We are cleansed, forgiven saints who "stumble in many ways" (James 3:2). We are no longer defined by our sin, but by God's Son. That's why we are saints. We aren't what we do. Yes, we still sin, but God has separated who we are from what we do. We were sinners and we are saved by grace alone, but that's not the end of the story. We're saints who have been saved, transformed, and made new by grace. This is the full gospel. It's not humility to call yourself something God doesn't. Biblical humility is agreeing with God even when you don't feel it. That's what it means to walk by faith and not by sight.

I recognize that so often it can feel like we are dirty, sinful people. I can feel that way too. But I don't have to feel something in order for it to be true. I don't always feel Christ in me, but I can know that He promises to never leave me. It's truth, not feelings, that we need to base our identity on. The reason understanding our identity in Christ matters is because we are going to live out what we believe. If I believe I am a sinner, then I am going to live that way. But if I believe I am a saint, a new creation with Christ living in me, then I am going to start living like who I am.

Just like the childhood nicknames—if I believe I'm stupid, fat, unworthy of love—then eventually every decision I make is going to run through that filter. But if I start realizing that God has changed me, why would I want to sin? It doesn't fit with who I am anymore.

You have a new name: *Saint*. You don't have to prove that you're a human; you simply are one. You were born a human. You were reborn a saint, a child of God. You don't have to prove your name; you just have it. It's a gift. It's part of being in a family. I'm a Maldonado forever. And you're a saint, God's child, righteous and holy—forever.

This is the foundation of our behavior. The New Testament teaches us to know our identity first so that we can live out who we really are in Christ. Paul illustrates this clearly when he says, "So, as those who have been chosen of God, holy and beloved, put on a heart of compassion, kindness, humility, gentleness and patience" (Colossians 3:12). We can live holy, compassionate, kind, gentle, and patient lives because Christ lives in us and because He's made us new creations who actually desire what He desires.

Beliefs are important. What we believe determines how we live and the actions we take. If I wrongly believe that my wife is cheating on me—even if she isn't—I wouldn't trust her and I would act out of that wrong belief. Likewise, if I believe I'm a sinner—though I'm not—I'm going to act out of a wrong belief.

You're Enough in Christ

One of the biggest lies I've believed is *I'm not enough*. Whether it was my past sin that screamed at me, "You're impure!" "You're unlovable!" "You don't have what it takes!" or "You will always be alone!" or years of having a misplaced identity, this is something I still have to reject each day. But the truth can set us free. As we awaken our minds to God's truth and start allowing His Spirit in us to live from that truth, we can find healing and freedom.

The truth is, you're adequate, you're enough, and you lack nothing in Christ. Colossians 2:10 says you're complete. Second Corinthians 3:6 says you are adequate to minister God's new covenant, and 2 Corinthians 2:15 says you are the pleasing aroma of God. Once we start believing in who God says we are, it allows us to finally live free from the burden of our past.

In Christ, we are forgiven and perfectly cleansed forever (Hebrews 10:14). This means nothing in our past can undo what Christ has done. In Christ, we are chosen, set apart, and dearly loved (Colossians 3:12). God's love can break the lie that says we aren't worthy to be loved. God's grace can break the lie that says we're not adequate or qualified. And God's eternal presence in us can break the lie that says we're lacking.

Renewing our mind is about taking the thoughts we entertain and putting them to the test with God's Word. If you're like me, your life has been spent performing. In school, it was working hard to earn a better grade or to become a starter in your sport or activity. At work, it was about impressing the boss or earning a promotion. With relationships, it was constantly needing to perform in order for people to like you.

Why do we do this, naturally? It's because we don't believe we're enough. We fear failure. We think if we fail, that makes us a failure. We have believed the lie that we have to achieve certain standards in order to feel like we're okay. We think our approval and worth comes from the opinion of others.

The bad news about performing for acceptance and performing for self-worth is that you never truly arrive. When you have to perform for acceptance, you jump on a treadmill. If you've ever been on a treadmill, you know that you can burn a lot of calories, sweat a lot, and get nowhere. Literally, you're running in place. This is like life. You may have some successes and be able to perform for a while, but eventually you realize you're not going anywhere. You still feel miserable. And like you're not enough.

God has totally accepted you and made you right with Him forever (Romans 15:7; 5:1). Nothing can change this. We live our entire lives from God's acceptance and approval of us. God delights in you and is pleased with who you are because you are His child (Zephaniah 3:17; 2 Corinthians 2:15). Do you see that everything we search for, we already have in Christ? Approval, love, worth, significance, companionship—we have all of that unconditionally in Christ.

This isn't an overnight fix. You need time and constant truth to begin dissolving old mindsets and beliefs and experiencing the freedom you already have. I've spent the last nine years doing more unlearning than learning. I'm unlearning all that religion and legalism has taught me. Your thoughts can be messy, but you're not messy. You're a masterpiece. We wouldn't ask someone with a broken wrist to be more disciplined in or to hurry their recovery. Their healing takes time. And so does ours.

Set Your Mind

Angry, gossiper, rude, weird, unworthy, broken, ugly, fat, stupid. So many of the labels you have given yourself, or that someone else has given you, are not true. Let's ask God to start replacing those lies with the truth of who you are. He is inviting you to set your mind on truth. As you set your mind, you choose truth, and as you choose truth, your emotions will begin aligning with that truth.

Colossians 3:1–2 tells us to set our minds on the things above, not on the things that are on Earth. This means we are to set our mind on where we are, whose we are, and what God says about us. We are raised and seated with Christ in heaven (Colossians 3:1; Ephesians 2:6). That's right, you're seated with Christ. Literally hidden in Him (Colossians 3:3). So, in the midst of fear, accusation, and chaos, we can choose to set our mind on the security and location of where we are. We are safe in God's embrace. And nothing, not even the evil one, can touch us (1 John 5:18).

We are God's children! We are His people forever. We are His possession (1 Peter 2:10). We are cared for and loved and never forsaken by God. In the midst of anxious, lonely, or negative thoughts, you can set your mind on the truth of our heavenly Father. He loves you. He is for you. And He is not ashamed of you!

The lies about who you are will come. Each time you sin, fail, or disappoint someone, they will come. Whether it's body image, your job, or your past, you can have an answer to the lies you hear. You're perfectly and wonderfully made (Psalm 139:14; Hebrews 10:14). You're blameless and at peace with God (Colossians 1:22; Romans 5:1). You're born of God, anointed, holy, sealed by the Spirit, redeemed, forgiven, and beloved (1 John

5:18; 2:27; Hebrews 10:10; Ephesians 1:13; Colossians 1:14; Ephesians 5:1).

God wants us to be consumed with His Son, not our sins. He wants us focused on who He says we are, not on what others say we are. Hebrews 12:2 tells us to "[fix] our eyes on Jesus, the pioneer and perfecter of faith" (NIV). Don't be so preoccupied with your past, your sins, or your shame. Be preoccupied with Jesus. He's enough. And His opinion is better than any hurt, shame, sin, or struggle you will ever face.

I love sneakers. I'm usually rocking a pair of Jordan 1s when I speak. I once bought (copped) a pair of Jordan 1s for $170 and turned around and sold them for over $1,000. Isn't that crazy? People see huge value in these shoes and are willing to pay almost ten times the retail value just to have a pair.

The way these shoes lose value is by being worn. And what I've noticed is that we think the same thing about ourselves. We believe that since we've been through a lot, been worn down by life, we've lost value. The good news of your identity is that you can never lose your value. You're priceless, and there's nothing you can do to change the value God has given you!

CHAPTER 17

He's Our Friend

"No longer do I call you slaves, for the slave does not know
what his master is doing; but I have called you friends."
John 15:15

Why is it that we can have hundreds or thousands of friends and followers on social media and still feel so alone? Or that we can be at an event, a party, a class, or work and feel alone and unseen? Researchers and scholars call us the "connected generation" because we are the most connected group of people to ever exist. And yet research shows we feel alone—a lot.

I was single for what felt like forever. Through most of high school and college I never had a relationship that stuck. I always wanted one but never had one that lasted. My singleness made me feel lonely. And my loneliness only enhanced the lie that I wasn't enough for anyone to love me or want me. If you're single, please know that you're enough. That singleness is not a curse. You're not less-than for being single.

You are complete in Christ, which means you can be happy and satisfied while being single. You have the fullness of God living in you, and He alone is able to meet every need you will ever have.

I was alone. In the middle of a South Texas ranch. Coyotes, man-killing hogs, and rattlesnakes were all around me. (I can't confirm if the hogs ever killed a man, but I'm sure they could.) One morning I was hunting with my dad and brother, and my dad left me in the middle of a pasture to take my brother to his stand. I was freaking out. It was dark. I could feel the breath of the coyotes breathing down my neck. Or maybe that was just fear. Either way, it was scary. And the coyotes were howling.

I guess I should mention that my dad left me with a loaded rifle and a pistol, and he probably was only a few hundred yards away. Nonetheless, fear gripped me. I was safe, but I didn't feel safe. I didn't feel like I was secure. I didn't feel protected.

It's crazy how darkness makes everything seem scarier. In darkness, every shadow looks like and every noise sounds like a monster. Fear itself is like darkness. It tricks us into believing things are there when they really aren't. Light exposes the false narratives of darkness. Fear creates a narrative that convinces us of things that aren't really true.

We all fear abandonment. Once you've experienced it, you almost come to expect it. I don't know how many times I've been ghosted (that's when someone just stops talking to you for no reason and they don't tell you). I had that experience a few times through high school and college, and it just added to the belief that I wasn't enough and wasn't worthy of love.

When we're lonely, fear convinces us that no one cares about us, that we will be abandoned forever. Fear is a liar. Loneliness is a feeling, not a fact. As believers, you and I are never truly alone, since Christ is always with us. Jesus is leading us to choose this truth, believe this truth, and then start living out this truth in every moment. Jesus enjoys being our Friend. He loves living in us. He enjoys us and He will never, ever refuse or reject us.

One of my new favorite verses comes from a story in Mark 9 about a father whose son was possessed by a demon. The father cried out, "I do believe; help my unbelief" (v. 24). This is our journey too. There will be moments when you believe Jesus is in you, and there will be (many) moments you need Him to help you believe. It's God's full-time job to convince you that He is in you always. It's His heart's desire to help you.

Remember: It's not about feeling the presence of God within you. It's about knowing that no matter what you feel, God is fully present—all the time.

United to Jesus

The core message of the gospel is that Christ is in you. The first message God gave humanity, when sending down His Son, was "God is with you." That's Jesus's name—Immanuel, meaning "God with us." For Him to not be with you would mean He would cease to exist. Many of us have believed a partial gospel. We thought the gospel was just about being forgiven and going to heaven one day. But the rest of the gospel is that Christ has joined Himself to you, right here and now.

First Corinthians 6:17 says we are one spirit with the Lord, and Romans 6:5 says we are united to Him. Many people try to compare our relationship with God to relationships we have with other people, but it falls short because our relationship with Jesus is closer than any other relationship we could ever have. We are literally one with Jesus. Jesus prayed for this union in John 17, and His prayer was answered. This is why Paul tells us we are hidden with Christ, we are seated with Christ, and Christ lives in us (Colossians 3:3; Ephesians 2:6; Galatians 2:20).

I hear it all the time: "I want to get closer to God." And I understand what most people mean. They mean they want to know Jesus more. But so often, Christians think that their relationship with God is about slowly achieving closeness to God, when the goal of the Christian life isn't to get closer to God. The goal is to know Him and know how close He already is (Philippians 3:9). We're as close to Jesus right now as we can ever possibly be.

Nothing can separate our union. We're one with Him. And He promises to never leave us. Someone might ask, "Can't we lose fellowship with God?" No. This is a perfect example of humans trying to make our relationship with God like our earthly friendships. We are seated with Christ in heaven (Ephesians 2:6) and we have been brought near by Christ's blood (Ephesians 2:13). Our closeness to God is based on God's work, not ours. So we can't mess it up. God has cleared out His entire day just to be with you. You don't have to feel the pressure of "making time for God." He has made time for you and will be with you all day, every day.

Nowhere in the New Testament does it talk about us going in and out of fellowship with Christ. Instead, Paul tells us that God has called us into fellowship with His Son (1 Corinthians 1:9).

Our feelings are not indicators of truth. God's Word is. Even though I felt like I wasn't safe and protected in the middle of that South Texas ranch, surrounded by coyotes, I was. I had the guns. I was safe. I was secure. God's presence in us is a fact, not a feeling. It's true, no matter what we may experience day to day.

Backsliding into Grace

I used to think the focus of the Christian life was serving God. But do you realize that Jesus came to serve and not be served (Matthew 20:28)? The beginning point of our relationship with Christ is receiving, not achieving. It's about letting Christ do for us what we could never do on our own. Sure, we serve Him and do good works, but these are not the foundation of our faith. Jesus is.

When Jesus resurrected from the dead, He didn't give some long speech or ask His faithless disciples to bow down and serve Him. He made them breakfast (John 21:9–14). This picture of Jesus perfectly captures who our God is. He's not needy. He's not served by human hands (Acts 17:25). I'm sorry to break it to you, but God doesn't need you. Take that in for a second. He doesn't need you, but He does want you. That's why He created this world, went to the cross, and rose again. He did it all for you! He wants you. He wants relationship with you. It's really that simple.

Many of us fear that we can somehow "backslide." It's a popular word in churches today, but it's nowhere to be found in the New Testament. God's friendship with us has no strings attached. Hebrews 7:25 says that Jesus "is able also to save forever those who draw near to God through Him." And Philippians 1:6 says, "He who began a good work in you will perfect it until the day of Christ Jesus." It's God's work to save us and keep us saved. Jude 24 says this clearly: "Now to him who is able to keep you from stumbling and to present you blameless before the presence of his glory with great joy" (ESV).

You see, in this world, when we fail, we fall into rejection, punishment, and shame. But when we fail with God, we fall into His acceptance, love, and grace. We never fall into punishment or shame with Him. Never.

Our Need for Each Other

Jesus is enough. We need each other. We need community. The first "not good" in Scripture was from God when He looked at Adam and said it wasn't good for him to be alone. God reveals His presence, His love, and His grace powerfully in community. My friend John Lynch says this about true community: "What if there was a place so safe that the worst of me could be known, and I would discover that I would not be loved less, but more in the telling of it?"[48]

This is the community God wants for you. I'm not talking about an accountability partner whom you compete with or who shames you for sinning each week. I'm talking about a group of people who will give you the freedom to be yourself—a group of people who will allow you to take off your mask and be loved. Maybe it's just a best friend for a while, but eventually try to find a group in your local community and church. Maybe start one. Have dinner, play golf, talk, go through a book—just have community. It doesn't have to be a Bible study. You could play a board game. Just be around people. The Enemy would love to isolate us and convince us that we don't need people.

It's not going to be easy. It takes work to build relationships with community. You have to take the time to earn people's trust and build trust with others. But there are believers around you who want to bear your burdens and encourage you, care for you, and love you. You don't have to do this life alone. Reach out, go get coffee, engage with people, and find the group that works for you.

Stop Trying

I wish I had the feelings too. But that's not the promise of the gospel. I want to feel His presence all the time. I want to feel His care and His love. I get it. But we need to stop trying to feel God's presence. We need to stop trying to impress Him. We need to stop trying to do anything to make Him love us more. Instead, let's start trusting.

We need to stop trying to please God. Instead, we need to trust He's already pleased. Second Corinthians 2:15 says, "We are to God the pleasing aroma of Christ" (NIV). Here's the paradox of this: by faith we are already pleasing to God, *and* we can please God. This is why Hebrews 11:6 says that "without faith it is impossible to please Him." If our focus is on pleasing God, eventually we will be convinced that we need to "keep God pleased." But that's not the goal or the focus. Instead, we need to realize that God "take[s] great delight" in us (Zephaniah 3:17 NIV).

Did you know that before Jesus started His earthly ministry, before He did a single miracle, God declared to the world that Jesus was His beloved Son in whom He was pleased? God was pleased with Jesus long before He fed the five thousand, healed a leper, or rose from the dead. God was pleased with Jesus because Jesus was His child, not because of what Jesus did.

The same is true of us. God's delight and pleasure rests on us because we are His children. God is pleased because we are His kids, not because we perform or behave well.

Servants work hard to please their master. Children don't. Servants work for their position. Children are in the family and live from their position. Children know their relationship isn't based on what they do for each other. And our relationship with God is rooted in His love for us, not our love for

Him. We can lighten up knowing that God smiles when He thinks of us. He thinks I'm His favorite, and He thinks you're His favorite too!

What I'm trying to say is, don't put the cart before the horse. Many jump to serving God and doing good works and getting busy for God without realizing the foundation and focus of our faith. It's not on us and what we need to do. It's on Jesus and what He's done. We need to remember that we don't obey to be accepted. We are accepted and loved, therefore we obey. We love Jesus not in order to achieve status with Him but because of His outrageous love for us. Our lives are simply a response to what's already been done, not an attempt to earn anything from Him.

The fruit of us not trying so hard to please God and focusing on trusting Him is that we will really start to please Him. It's a simple change of focus, but it could change everything for you!

PART 5

BETTER THAN YOUR CIRCUMSTANCES

"You have for yourselves a better and lasting possession."

Hebrews 10:34

"I have learned to be content whatever the circumstances."

Philippians 4:11

CHAPTER 18

He's Our Rest

"Stop striving and know that I am God."
Psalm 46:10

One of the most popular cars in the early twentieth century, the Model T, didn't have a gas gauge. Drivers didn't know when they would run out of gas, which is why you would often see Fords on the side of the road. Isn't that wild? They would just have to guess at how much gas they had or get out and use a ruler or stick to measure it.

That illustration describes so many of us. We just go and go and go without any idea of when we're going to burn out and run out. Days off, vacations, naps—nothing seems to help. We're worn out. Exhausted. And running on empty.

I'm the world's worst. I can be a perfectionist and a workaholic, and I regularly find myself looking for approval by pleasing people. We're addicted to work because we think it can one day give us rest or fulfillment. We think doing more and trying harder is our answer to lasting peace. And sometimes, we let this attitude affect our relationship with Jesus.

To this day, every time I stay the night with my little brother, it's a fight to get him to sleep. For whatever reason, some young kids hate the idea of sleep. They think they're going to miss out on something. I can be the same way. I have the tendency to fact-check everything—right before I go to sleep. Instead of just drifting off, I start thinking about all kinds of stuff or worrying about tomorrow. It's not even just at bedtime. Many of us suffer from FOMO (fear of missing out) at other times. We hate scrolling through social media and seeing our friends having fun without us.

Maybe the reason we don't want to miss out on things is because we truly don't believe we are enough, we are accepted, and we are okay. I once spent forever searching all over my house for my cell phone, looking under every piece of furniture and in every pair of jeans to only discover *it was in my pocket the entire time*. You've probably done that with your keys or glasses too. The reality is, this is a picture of our lives. We are searching and seeking for something we *already have* in Christ.

We believe the lie of *more*. We need more money, more success, more approval, more likes, more followers, more, more, more. And haven't you noticed that it's never enough? This is why we're always in a hurry to do more. The solution isn't going to come from merely slowing down, working less, or taking longer vacations. Those things are great, but we need something more than that. We don't need principles, and we don't need rules. What we truly need is to discover the rest the Person of Jesus offers and how His reign in our life brings lasting rest.

What we need to do is recognize the burden is no longer on us. The burden of being accepted or loved or okay is not on us. The cross and resurrection means that the burden of working for God's love and acceptance and presence is over. We're already in. God's inviting us to recognize this and then just collapse in His arms and let Him carry us. The search is over and we're complete (Colossians 2:10).

Research has shown that 85 to 90 percent of the things we worry about don't come true.[49] God's got you. He's with you in all your worry. And since He takes care of the sparrows, He'll take care of you. You're of great value to Him. Even when you worry, God is faithful to you through it. You can stop trying to make everything work out and start resting in Jesus who's carrying you through till the end.

More Than a Day Off

While many people think a Sabbath day or a day off will help, that's not really Jesus's solution. The Sabbath in the Old Testament was only a shadow of God's true design. The true design is resting in Christ. The shadow was a day off; the actual thing is rest in Christ every single day (Colossians 2:16–17). Hebrews 4:9–10 tells us that our Sabbath rest is found in Jesus, not a day of the week. It's not that physical rest isn't good; it is. Take a day off or two. But what Jesus offers us is more than just physical. It's spiritual. And our spiritual rest in Christ will bring more physical rest than a day off ever will.

Adam and Eve showed up when all the work was done. Their first day was the Sabbath. They did nothing to help God create the universe. They simply showed up and enjoyed it. That was God's original design. He didn't want Adam and Eve to live *for* rest. He wanted them to live *from* rest. Their starting point was rest. When you got saved, did you do anything to help Jesus finish His work on the cross? Of course not. You showed up and the work was already done. Now you're invited to live from Jesus's finished work, not for it.

Okay, that sounds great, but what does this look like practically? Jesus promises us rest for our souls in Matthew 11:28–30. He says, "Come to me, all who labor and are heavy laden, and I will give you rest. Take my yoke upon you, and learn from me, for I am gentle and lowly in heart, and you will find rest for your souls. For my yoke is easy, and my burden is light" (ESV).

Jesus offers us Himself—not "five steps to rest" or a "four-fold path to peace" or a list of instructions to achieve rest for our souls. What is striking about this invitation is that He's actually inviting us to Himself to work.

The yoke was created for work, not rest. This imagery is drawn from two animals who share a wooden yoke that goes around their necks. When a smaller animal is learning, they team them up with a larger animal and the larger animal does all the work so that the smaller one can learn from the larger. Jesus is inviting us to take off the yoke that is burdening us and instead put on His. And when we put on His, He carries the burden.

His yoke and burden are easy and light. Why is that? Well, Jesus guides us and leads us. He teaches us, refreshes us, strengthens us, and equips us. He's the source! He's not merely giving us rest; instead, He is our rest. He's the source we draw from. No longer do we need to seek to gain rest from what we achieve; now we draw from our Source of rest, Jesus Christ. And we let Him do in us and through us what we could never do on our own.

Jesus will never ask you to do something that He hasn't equipped you to do. Furthermore, 1 Thessalonians 5:24 promises that "He who calls you is faithful; he will surely do it" (ESV). Christ is living in you and living through you as you trust in Him. Jesus isn't inviting us to do nothing. He's inviting us to recognize who we are, trust Him, and start living.

This plays out in our lives in a number of ways. First, we need to stop trying to do something that's already been done for us. So many of us are trying to earn our acceptance, achieve God's love, gain His forgiveness, and keep Him happy. That work has been done. Now the "work" is to believe in what's been done for you (John 6:29). Jesus nailed your sins on the cross and said, "It is finished," not "More work needs to be done."

This goes back to what I said earlier: we live from God's love, acceptance, and forgiveness, not for it. This means our entire life is spent obeying, serving, giving, and living from these truths, not for them. You can't defeat your struggle with sin, and God doesn't want *you* to. Jesus doesn't tell us to defeat sin; He invites us to rest in the victory over sin that He's already accomplished (1 Corinthians 15:57).

When we need love or patience or gentleness, we don't have to muster that up on our own. We get to draw from the source of love and patience and encouragement, Christ Himself. That's why it's called the fruit of the Spirit. It's not the fruit of our best effort.

Hebrews 10:12 tells us that Jesus sat down. In the Old Testament, no priest ever sat down. Ever. Why? Their work was never done. They constantly had to offer sacrifices in order to atone for the sins of the people. But after Jesus offered Himself, He sat down because His work was effective and done. Ephesians 2:6 says that we're seated with Christ too. Are you searching all over this world for something you already have? Are you working and hustling and trying to do something that's already been done? Can I invite you to recognize that the work has been done? Take a seat. It is finished.

Attention, Not Activity

There were sisters in the Bible named Martha and Mary. One day Jesus stopped in at their house to hang out. The women decided to do two different things. Martha chose to do things for Jesus, while Mary chose to sit at His feet. Most of us are Martha in this story. At least I am. I mean, I would be cleaning my house and trying to figure out what to cook and serve Jesus. Or I'd at least be trying to get my wife to cook something while I throw stuff in the closets. We can relate to Martha because we live in a nonstop world. We're always going. And we're always trying to impress others with what we do.

Martha was distracted with all that she was doing, and she asked Jesus, "Don't you care?" I love this because I've asked this of Jesus more times than I can count. Maybe you've done the same. The disciples did the same thing when they thought they were going to drown. Jesus was napping, and they woke Him up, asking, "Don't you care if we drown?" (Mark 4:38). It's okay to question God.

Jesus answers Martha by saying, "You're worried and anxious about a lot of things, but only one thing matters, and your sister has discovered it."

What did Mary discover? That resting at Jesus's feet is what matters. Jesus wants our attention more than He wants our activity. We've bought the lie that our focus needs to be on our sins. We're constantly sold a "sin-management" message—that we need to manage our sins and straighten up. But the more we focus on our sins, the more we sin. The Bible invites us to focus on Jesus, not our sins (Hebrews 12:1–2), because the more we focus on Jesus, the less we sin.

Jesus didn't say serving was bad. But He wants something better for us. The pressure to do good works for God should not be our motivation. God has already prepared us for good works (Ephesians 2:10). Our job is simply to be available to Him. The only way we can be available is if we're focused on Him. Think about it. If Jesus needed something, who would have been able to get it for Him—Mary or Martha? Mary, because she was attentive and right there at His feet.

"Cease striving and know that I am God" (Psalm 46:10). Stop striving for God. The goal isn't to spend your life striving for Him. The goal is to know Jesus. The fruit of knowing Jesus is that we bear much fruit. Paul said in Colossians 2:21–23 that rules have the appearance of wisdom but give us no power over sin. It's only Jesus that can lead us and teach us to say no to sin, not rules or our best effort.

Jesus is our anchor. Have you thought about what that means? If you've ever seen a boat anchored in the water, you know that the boat can drift side to side, but the anchor won't let it go beyond a certain point. Our soul is like the boat. It can experience all kinds of things, but no matter what, it's anchored. It's secure. No matter what it feels day to day, it's anchored. We can feel good and we can feel bad, but no matter what, our hope is steady and secure. And our hope and anchor is Jesus.

Growth Is from God

I've never been in a vineyard and heard the branches struggling or striving, have you? Jesus is the vine and we are the branches (John 15:5). We don't produce the fruit; we just bear it. It's the fruit of the Spirit, not the fruit of our striving (Galatians 5). Take a breath. The pressure is off you. Our growth is from God alone (Colossians 2:19; 1 Corinthians 3:7). It's God's plan to conform us to His Son (Romans 8:29).

Jesus is perfectly God, perfect in everything, yet we read that He grew in wisdom and that He learned obedience (Luke 2:52; Hebrews 5:8). We're complete and righteous, yet we're learning about who God has made us to be, and we're learning how to live from our new identity and not from our old habits. In the same way that a baby doesn't get more human as it grows up, you and I don't get holier, more accepted, or more complete as we mature. Instead, we just learn to be who we are.

The Bible says we grow—through Jesus, not through self-effort (Colossians 2:6). Remember, you're complete in Christ (Colossians 2:10). You have everything you need for life and godliness (1 Peter 1:3). And you are blessed with every spiritual blessing (Ephesians 1:3). Stop striving to grow or mature. Just know God and He will take care of the rest.

CHAPTER 19

He Fights for Us

"The Lord will fight for you; you need only to be still."
Exodus 14:14 NIV

You're not less of a Christian or a person if you struggle with anxiety, depression, or any mental illness. If you're struggling, please reach out to someone—your pastor, your best friend, whomever—and please seek help (your doctor or a mental health professional can help you determine the best steps). It's okay to seek professional help. There's been a stigma on this topic in Christian circles, and we need to know that it's normal and okay to need help.

The message of this chapter is that God is in the middle of your anxiety, depression, and struggle, relentlessly fighting for you to believe that you are enough, loved, cared for, and protected. He's fighting for you to know that He's got you and that He doesn't think any less of you. Our fight is not to get forgiven, get free, or be made new. The fight is to believe those things are already true. And in the midst of our struggle, the fight isn't to become enough, earn love, or get God's attention; instead, God's fighting for you to realize the truth of who you are and who He is to you in those moments.

That's why it's so important to realize our identity in Christ, because when we do we can properly understand that we are not the problem. Sadly, many Christians believe that they are the problem and that, in order to break free from depression or any sin, they have to look within and figure out what's wrong with them. But we all have negative feelings and thoughts, and we need to know that the source of those feelings, thoughts, and temptations is not us. They come from this broken world, the Enemy, and the power of sin.

You're not alone in this struggle. In the Bible, Hannah experienced bitterness of soul over infertility and a broken domestic situation. Elijah felt so beaten down that he asked God to take his life. In Psalms, David repeatedly asked his own soul why it was so downcast. Even Jesus expressed that His soul was overwhelmed with sorrow, even to the point of death.

Although there are some great Bible passages on what to do when anxiety and thoughts strike, the thing that has helped me most in times of anxiety, depression, or some other mental struggle is knowing that God is not passive. He's active. He's fighting. He's working for you and me. God is not far off; He's in it with us. His voice, presence, and protection are greater than any evil in this world (1 John 4:4). Know this: God will never get tired of sustaining you or comforting you or weeping with you or loving you. It is His ultimate desire to love you.

Throughout different seasons of my life, I've struggled with negative thinking, depression, and anxiety. What I keep coming back to is truth—the truth about Christ in me and who He has made me to be, the truth about His affection and care for me, and the truth that my life matters and that I have value and purpose in Him.

It's helpful if we look at lies surrounding mental illness in order to get a clearer view of the truth of what God is doing and what He thinks of us.

Lies vs. Truths

The first lie is that true believers don't struggle with depression, anxiety, worry, hurt, or any other mental health issue. The truth is that these things are unavoidable, and because we live in a broken world, we will all experience them. No struggle diminishes God's opinion of you or your status as a believer. We are saved by grace—not by whether or not we struggle—and we're kept by grace, not by our perfect emotions or behavior. If true believers didn't struggle, there wouldn't be any need for the countless verses that encourage us not to worry, fear, or be anxious. Jesus told us that we would face trouble of all kinds, but our hope is in the fact that no matter what we face, Christ has overcome the world (John 16:33).

The second lie is that believers "just need more faith." As we discussed earlier, faith is a gift from God. You've got all the faith you need. You lack nothing. God never promises us perfect emotions or circumstances. The Bible doesn't guarantee us perfect health and emotions if we just believe better or harder or more. The truth is that a mental illness is not your fault. God isn't blaming you.

As a friend of mine says, it's okay to have Jesus and a therapist. You're complete in Christ. So ditch the lie that says you're the problem. Paul told Timothy to take some wine for his stomach ailments (1 Timothy 5:23), not to "have more faith." You are enough.

The next lie is subtle and tricky. It claims that if you read the Bible more and pray more, then you'll feel better. People can say this with good intentions, but it's not the real answer. Our hope isn't in reading or praying; our hope is in Christ. Although these things are helpful and can be powerful tools to help renew our minds and bring healing, it may also be good to see a counselor and/or take medication.

As a pastor, I believe the truth of Scripture can set us free and bring so much healing and peace in our lives. But God uses all sorts of things to bring healing to us. We wouldn't tell someone who had a broken leg to just pray more or read their Bible; they need a medical doctor. Sometimes, a person who struggles with depression or anxiety has a chemical imbalance or a biological issue that needs to be addressed.

The next lie has already been touched on, but it bears repeating because many of us still believe it. The lie is that your struggle is punishment from God. The truth is, God is good. Period. And He's good to you. He is not punishing you. There's no punishment left (Romans 8:1). The cross was enough for you. It worked. God is for you.

If you believe this lie because you think it's due to a "sin" in your life, you need to realize that God is not relating to us based on our sin or performance. God relates to us based on the cross and resurrection. He's taken your sins away. He'll never turn His back on you or ditch you. Your sins don't surprise God. He saw all your sins and has chosen to love and be with you forever.

The last lie we will look at says that if you were more spiritually mature, you wouldn't struggle." The truth is that your struggle is never because you're not enough or because God doesn't love you. Christian maturity is not about becoming strong and independent. No, true Christian maturity is about realizing how weak and dependent you are. It's about growing more dependent upon God, not less.

We never grow out of our need of God's grace. We only grow deeper into our need of it. If we really are complete, lacking nothing and with everything we need for life and godliness, then our struggle is not because we are not mature. The Bible says we have an enemy, we have the power of sin at work, and we have this fallen world that is throwing all kinds of things at us.

Perhaps that's what we need to know the most: there's an enemy at work in this world. He can't touch us (1 John 5:18), but he loves to tempt us and distract us. There's also this parasite called sin crouching at our door (Genesis 4:7). It feeds us thoughts and lies about God and who we are. And then there's the flesh. The flesh isn't the old you; the old you was crucified and buried. You're only one you, the new creation. The flesh is a term for all those old thoughts and beliefs and ways we used to find fulfillment.

It's important to recognize that we have an enemy. And the enemy is not us. We are on God's side in this equation. Our fight is not against some "evil part of us." You are not depression, you are not sin, and you are not your thoughts. You're a child of God who wrestles with these things.

I asked my friend John Lynch why depression, anxiety, and mental struggles happen. He said, "For some, the struggle is temporary. For others, irregular. For some, the struggle never goes away. For some, it seems to have ended, then returns. For many it is chemical or biological. For some, the result of chronic pain. For some, because of grief or loss. For some, the result of ongoing personal wounding. For some, the result of sexual abuse. For many, it is the result of bad theology. For some, sleep disorders. For some, postpartum complications. For some, the result of unforgiveness. For some, the result of some tension in life. For many, there is absolutely no apparent basis. It just happens."

In light of that, I hope you realize that you are not a project to be fixed. You are a person to be loved. You are safe. You don't need to hide. You are not the exception. You are not alone in this struggle. I need you as much as you need me. That's why I'm urging you, whether you struggle or not, to be in community and to get help. Many of us aren't prepared to love others well, and that's okay. We're learning. And we can teach each other how to love better.

God Is Good to You

God's not playing some game with you. As I said earlier, many theologies basically say God is playing good cop/bad cop with us. We think God is throwing pain our way and then coming to us and comforting us. Nope. God is good to us. Does He allow the pain? Yes. But is He the source of our pain? No. He doesn't cause it. God's not playing with us. He's not far off, asking us to figure this out all on our own. And He hasn't moved on to someone else. His entire schedule has your name written on it. You're His full-time job.

God doesn't ask us to get past it or get over it. Never. He's inviting us to trust Him with every problem and struggle that comes our way. Even when we are faithless, God remains faithful. All of His promises are held up by His faithfulness and commitment and dedication to you; not by your faithfulness, commitment, or dedication to Him.

Suicide is not the unforgivable sin, nor is suicide the sin that leads to death. The sin leading to death (the unforgivable sin) is the rejection of the gospel and the rejection of Jesus Christ as Lord and Savior (1 John 5:16). That is why John says we should not pray for it because our prayer cannot turn someone to God (1 John 5:17). Only the Holy Spirit can do that. Further, the entire letter of 1 John is dedicated to contrasting those who are saved and those who are not.

To say that God sends a believer to hell because they made the choice to kill themselves totally misses the heart of God. Nowhere in Scripture does it say suicide is an unforgivable sin or that suicide is different from any other sin. Our forgiveness is not rooted in how little or small our sins are; our forgiveness is based on the shed blood of Jesus. There is no such thing as big sins and small sins, just sins. And Jesus took them all away.

So if you've lost someone to suicide, please see and know the heart of your Father. He is good, all the time. We need to start seeing God as good and stop seeing Him through the lens of our shame and the religious teaching we grew up with.

A Way Forward

As many of us know, depression can feel like a heavy fog. Anxiety can paralyze you or make you feel like everything is about to blow up in your face. Whether you struggle with anxiety or depression or neither, we all face seasons of sadness and emotional turmoil. In my own life, this is true. Counseling and talking to friends and being in community are all valuable, and there are also some truths that I love to lean on in seasons when I feel anxious or sad.

Jesus says we don't have to be anxious because He's got us. He is the beginning and the end. He's seen everything that has happened and will happen to you. Your sin and anxious thoughts and everything that has happened in your life have not caught Him by surprise. He wants us to share with Him what is causing us to worry, doubt, fear, and be sad. Think of it like this: We're carrying our burdens around in a bag. God is asking us to give Him the things that weigh us down, and as we take the items (our worries) out of our bag and give them to Him, we are "casting our cares" on Him. We can cast our cares on God because He really does care for us (1 Peter 5:7). And He promises to be our peace. God is inviting us to humbly trust in His care for us by asking for our cares. He's in you, and He deeply cares for you.

I sometimes think I annoy my wife with my constant needs. But again and again, she loves me and cares for me and reminds me that she is never burdened by, bothered by, or tired of my going to her. She loves to care for me. She loves to love me. How much more does God love to care and love us in our times of need? God promises us that the Spirit inside us will bring to remembrance all that Jesus has taught us (John 14:26). So we can be confident that in the midst of our mess, God is working in us.

One last thing. I've been trying to wake up each morning and give thanks. It's simple. But sometimes I don't want to do it. But it's helped me—a lot. Studies show that gratitude improves mental health, and people who practice it are often happier.[50] Knowing that God is for me and that He forgives me, loves me, will never forsake me, and has given me everything I need for life and godliness, gives me a lot of reasons to be thankful.

Take a moment and give God thanks for all He's done for you.

CHAPTER 20

He Frees Us

"If the Son sets you free, you really will be free."
John 8:36

One of the most freeing things for me on my journey of discovering that Jesus is better is the truth that we really are free. The goal of the cross and resurrection was freedom, not bondage. Christianity should feel like your chains have been broken and the weight is off, not bondage and slavery. Paul says in Galatians 5:1, "It is for freedom that Christ has set us free. Stand firm, then, and do not let yourselves be burdened again by a yoke of slavery" (NIV). The freedom Paul most talks about is our freedom from the law.

In my own life, this freedom has led to freedom *from* sin. It's led to me trusting Jesus more and doing more for Him, not less. But it's because of His love, not for it. It's based on love, not a fear of messing up. When my focus changed from what I need to do for God to what Christ has done for me, everything changed. I now focus more on Jesus, His work, and His life in me. This shift in focus has made all the difference.

For whatever reason, we're scared of freedom, and pastors and teachers can be the worst about this. How many times have we heard, "It's great you're saved, but you better get to work and serve, serve, serve"? There's a lot of double-talk when it comes to our freedom—a lot of "Yeah, but …" It's no wonder so many people think Christianity is about following rules. But Jesus didn't come to put us under more rules; He came to set us free.

Haven't you noticed that on July 4th—or any other day—Americans don't fly British flags or have King George III statues to celebrate and honor? We celebrate our freedom from the tyranny that once bound us. For Christians, that tyranny was the law. Many of you may be thinking, *Of course, Zach. That's Christianity 101.* But let me take it a step further. God set us free from the Ten Commandments too. These ten are the law.

I'm not alone in believing this. It's actually quite the debate among theologians, whether we are under the law or not and exactly what that means for believers. Many leading New Testament scholars agree that the purpose of the law has been accomplished and therefore believers are no longer bound by the Ten Commandments or any part of the Mosaic Law.[51]

It seems clear to me that the New Testament teaches this, but before we look at that, I want to stress a few things. I'm not saying the Old Testament isn't the inspired Word of God. It is, and we can learn from it. We can read the Old Testament law all while wearing polyester, eating bacon, and working on Saturday. Furthermore, in saying believers are free from the law, I'm not saying I'm "anti-law" or "antinomian." I am saying I'm pro-Jesus and pro-context. I'm not hating on the law; instead, I'm just placing it in its proper context.

We cannot pick and choose from the law. We're free from it. The only way to live free from sin and to live in the freedom Jesus bought us is to trust Jesus for everything, not just forgiveness. Jesus is better than anything the law offers us. And my goal is to point people to Jesus, not tablets of stone.

The book of Hebrews makes this clear: "For, on the one hand, there is a setting aside of a former commandment because of its weakness and uselessness (for the Law made nothing perfect), and on the other hand there is a bringing in of a better hope, through which we draw near to God" (Hebrews 7:18-19 ESV). Hebrews 8:13 says, "When He said, 'A new covenant,' He has made the first obsolete." This is why the New Covenant is described as better over and over again.

The law was only a "shadow of the good things to come" (Hebrews 10:1). The good has come. His name is Jesus. We need to trust His sacrifice for our forgiveness, His resurrection life for our salvation, and His indwelling Spirit for our daily living. That's the message of this book—that we can trust Jesus from start to finish.

It should be obvious by now, but I need to say this as well: Jesus will never lead a person to murder or steal or commit adultery or disrespect their parents or sin. But to say we still need the Ten Commandments as our guide is to disregard Christ in us, or to say the law is better than Jesus. We don't need the law or the Ten Commandments for our morality. Jesus is our morality. We don't need the law to guide us. Jesus in us is our guide. Jesus is enough to produce love, ethics, and morality in us and through us.

Yes, some of the commandments are repeated throughout the New Testament. But this just shows us that God's character hasn't changed. Nonetheless, we don't find our source of morality in the Ten Commandments. That would mean working on the Sabbath is sin. Instead, we trust Christ and let Him be our source of morality. We let the New Covenant speak about what guides us and what love ultimately looks like when it's expressed in our lives.

Paul gives us plenty of instructions on what love and trusting Jesus look like. There are behavior passages and commands found all throughout the New Testament. But the difference between those and Old Testament law is the foundation. Under the Old Covenant, we obeyed in order to get blessed, but under the New Covenant, we obey because of what Christ has done for us and by His power in us.

We forgive because God has forgiven us (Ephesians 4:32; Colossians 3:13). We love because God has loved us. We live holy because God has made us holy. Under the Old Covenant, obedience was the cause of God's love and blessings. Under the New Covenant, obedience is the fruit of the love and blessing God has already poured out on us.

Jesus Fulfilled the Law

Jesus came to do for us what we could never do on our own. He came and fulfilled the perfect standards of the law. He did this to satisfy the requirements of the law so that He could bring in the New Covenant (see Romans 8:3–4). Galatians 4:4–5 tells us, "When the set time had fully come, God sent His Son, born of a woman, born under law, to redeem those under law, that we might receive the full rights of sons" (NIV). Jesus was born under the law to fulfill it for us.

Romans 10:4 says, "Christ is the end of the law for righteousness to everyone who believes." Whether Paul means "end" or "goal," the meaning is the same—the law points to Christ and the law finds it's ending at Christ. This is why Jesus tells us that He didn't come to do away with the law, but to fulfill it (Matthew 5:17). You will find no verse in the New Testament that commands believers to obey or fulfill the law of Moses. None. We don't have to do something that Jesus has already done.

There's a clear difference between law and grace. John 1:17 helps us see this: "For the Law was given through Moses; grace and truth were realized through Jesus Christ." As Galatians 3:24–25 says, the law led us to Christ, but now that we've been saved, we're no longer under the supervision of the law. In Christ, we have "died to the law" and been "released from the law" (Romans 7:4-6 ESV). Did you know that the only way to bear fruit and live for God is apart from the law (see Romans 7:4 and Galatians 2:19)? Romans 6:14 makes it clear: "You are not under law but under grace." Galatians 5:18 says the same thing: "You are not under the Law."

In Christ, we are completely and totally free from the law. He does what the law could never do: "And through Him everyone who believes is freed from all things, from which you could not be freed through the Law of Moses" (Acts 13:39).

The law is not for believers. Paul makes this clear in 1 Timothy 1:8– 10: "Law is made not for the righteous but for lawbreakers and rebels, the ungodly and sinful, the unholy and irreligious" (NIV). The law came in to show that everyone was a prisoner of sin and to silence us and make us conscious of sin (Romans 3:19–20; Galatians 3:19–24).

Being free from the law is not just about justification. Everyone agrees that the law doesn't justify us, but we still think we need the law as our guide. Galatians 2:16 is clear that the law cannot justify anyone. But we can't pick and choose what parts of the law we want to obey or how we apply it. It's all or nothing. We're either totally free from the law or we're not.

The law was only a shadow; the true substance and reality is Christ (Colossians 2:17). To say that we're only under part of the law (the Ten Commandments) is to do something no New Testament writers did. You can't separate the Ten Commandments from the rest of the law. Many theologians try to separate the law into three categories, but the New Testament never does this.

James 2:10 says, "Whoever shall keep the whole Law, yet stumbles in one point, he is guilty of breaking all of it." Paul echoes the same thought in Galatians 5:3 when he says that if someone wants to be circumcised, they're obligated to keep the whole law.

The law "arouses sin" (Romans 7:5) and produces sinful desires in those who try to keep it (Romans 7:8). And "all who rely on observing the law are under a curse" (Galatians 3:10 NIV). Further, the law is a ministry of death. In 2 Corinthians 3:7, Paul says the Ten Commandments specifically is a ministry of death: "if the ministry that brought death, which was engraved in letters on stone." Only the Ten Commandments were engraved on stone. Do you see the clear picture?

This is why it's God's grace, not law, that teaches us to live godly and say no to sin (Titus 2:12). Paul discovered that apart from the law, sin had no power over him. Let's look at Romans 7:8 again: "But sin, taking opportunity through the commandment, produced in me coveting of every kind; for apart from the Law sin is dead." Coveting is one of the Ten Commandments. When Paul placed himself under the Ten, He didn't covet less, but more. So living under the law actually leads us to sin more, not less. That's why God's answer is for us to trust in His Spirit to lead us, teach us, guide us, and inspire us to live godly.

Freedom from sin is found when we live under grace, not law. Only grace can produce in us and through us what the law never could. Those who disagree with me on this issue don't disagree on the goal. The goal is the same—upright living and dependency on Christ. But the method is different. I'm saying the New Testament teaches that the method is God's grace, not law. The method is trust in Jesus from start to finish: "Therefore as you have received Christ Jesus the Lord, so walk in Him" (Colossians 2:6). We are led by God's Spirit, not the law (Romans 8:14; Galatians 5:18, 25).

Paul, after calling the Galatians foolish in Galatians 3, asks them a series of questions: "Did you receive the Spirit by observing the law, or by believing what you heard? Are you so foolish? After beginning with the Spirit, are you now trying to attain your goal by human effort?" (vv. 1–3). So he equates "human effort" with living by the law. Notice, this is about daily living. So we live the same way we began, by dependence on God's Spirit. That's the difference between the law and Jesus. Under the law, it's all about you and your effort. But under the New Covenant, we live by God's strength, His power, and His life in us.

I broke my thumb my senior year of high school. When I went to the doctor, they took an x-ray of my thumb, which confirmed that it was broken. But the x-ray machine couldn't fix my broken thumb; it could only reveal or expose the problem. The law is like an x-ray machine. It can show you what's broken, but it has no power to fix you.

The law cannot save, nor can it grow or empower a person. The law is holy and good, but it cannot make a person holy or good, nor can it empower holiness. The law only condemns, kills, and reveals our need for something better. The law is a perfect standard that no one can attain. When we place ourselves under the law as our guide or our source of morality and godly living, then we are setting ourselves up for failure, condemnation, and death.

We love to sing about how amazing the grace of God was to save us. But why stop there? If grace is powerful enough to save us, then it's powerful enough to teach us, guide us, and keep us from sinning.

Our focus doesn't need to be on "keeping the rules" or "obeying the Ten Commandments." Our focus needs to be on Jesus. Yes, there are still commands. First John 3:23 tells us what they are: "This is His commandment, that we believe in the name of His Son Jesus Christ, and love one another." This is the same thing Jesus commanded us in John 13:34. This is why "His commandments are not burdensome" (1 John 5:3).

His commandments are not Old Testament law, because if they were they'd be burdensome. We know that the law is a yoke no one can bear: "Why do you put God to the test by placing upon the neck of the disciples a yoke which neither our fathers nor we have been able to bear?" (Acts 15:10).

Living under grace doesn't mean obedience doesn't matter. It does! We've become obedient from the heart (Romans 6:17). The New Testament gives us plenty of instructions on how we are to live our lives. But they are all an expression of love. They come from our new heart and Christ in us. The New Testament calls this the "law of Christ" (1 Corinthians 9:21). And law here, contrary to Old Testament law, is more like a power or influence. We are now guided internally by the influence and power of Christ, who is love. This is why Paul says he's compelled by the love of Christ (2 Corinthians 5:14). And since our hearts have been filled with God's love, it's our desire to love (Romans 5:5).

You are free. You are free to trust Jesus for your behavior and morality. Your relationship with God is not law-based; it's love-based.

CHAPTER 21

He's Our Life

"When Christ, who is our life, is revealed, then you
also will be revealed with Him in glory."
Colossians 3:4

Driving after midnight is never a good idea. I was heading to meet my dad a few hours from where I lived so we could go deer hunting. It was the middle of the winter, and there was snow on the ground (rare for Texas) and ice on the roads. I set out shortly after midnight and was driving well below the speed limit. It amazed me how many people were passing me. Really, *passing* isn't accurate. They were flying by me!

Next thing I knew, my pickup lost traction. I had hit some black ice. I did a 180 and was heading for the ditch. As I looked out my side window, I saw that the ditch was flat and that there was a fence in the distance. I figured I could hit the fence with the side of my truck and it would save me without much damage to the truck since I was parallel with the fence. But just as I was thinking that—*boom!* My pickup hit a metal cable, the kind that runs from a wooden power pole into the ground for support.

Once I hit that black ice, I was out of control. There was nothing I could do to fix my current situation. A lot of times, this is what life feels like. Anxiety hits, a bad circumstance comes our way, and we feel like we're losing control and there's nothing we can do about it. We try our hardest to make life "work," and often there's nothing we can do to control what happens. A death, a lost job, a pandemic—all of these things feel like hitting black ice.

My pickup was totaled by that cable, but I was great. Not a scratch on me. This is the perfect picture of Christ being our life. We can feel like everything around us is spinning out of control, and we can wreck our circumstances by our decisions or just by life happening to us, and yet Christ will never leave us. Spiritually, we are safe and secure with Him. Our circumstances, our choices—nothing can cause Christ to leave us. Nothing can spiritually harm us. He's always working in us, no matter what's happening around us.

I love being organized. I love files and drawers and spreadsheets. And I've noticed that many of us treat God like one file among many. We have a file for our family and a file for our money and a file for our job and a file for our church. Lastly, we have a file for God. But God is not a file. God is the whole filing cabinet. God is our life. It's from Him that we live our life. Christ as our life shapes how we see and organize everything. We see it all through the lens of Christ as our life.

You don't go to work and leave God. God is in you at work, in your relationships, and in everything that you do.

No matter what happens day to day, we can know that our source of joy and peace is found in Him alone. It's not about having more faith in order to make our circumstances better, nor is it about doing more in order to be more victorious. Instead, it's simply about trusting Christ who is life to us even in the midst of bad circumstances.

I can lose everything in this world and it will never take away all that I have in Christ. The things of this world do not give me life. Only Jesus does, and He truly is enough. Having "more" is only a façade. Jesus truly is all we ever need.

One of the low points in my life happened when I was twenty. I was working two jobs and going to school full-time. I was barely able to pay my bills, and was chasing after better circumstances. I wanted healing, a girlfriend, more money, and the job of my dreams, and I couldn't understand why God wasn't giving any of them to me. I had bought into a subtle lie that Christianity is about making my circumstances and life better—and that if I had a little more faith, things would start happening for me.

That caused me to question God's goodness and my own faith. I started thinking God was sending bad things to "teach me a lesson." And that if I learned my lesson, then He would come through for me. Thankfully, I had some wise people around me whom God used to reveal something that made it all click: Christ is my life. He's not merely trying to make my life more comfortable. He is life to me in every moment, both in the comfortable and uncomfortable.

Christ is not merely our Savior, our Friend, our Teacher, and our Lord. He's our life. He is the source of our peace, happiness, joy, and existence. Our success, our job, our failures, our income, and even our day-to-day life is *not* our life. Christ is. He is the very thing that we live from and live for. This means we are no longer seeking to get anything from our circumstances, but instead we live from all that we already have in Christ.

Many of us believe that if we obey enough, study enough, or do more things for God, then He will do something for us—like fix our circumstance or bank account or make something grow or grant us our wish. That's us trying to manipulate God by doing for God so that God will do something for us. Whether we recognize it or not, that is the message we've often believed.

But there's something better! Christ is our life in every moment, and He is leading us and showing us in Scripture what life looks like when we trust Him in every moment. He's not our magic genie. He's our God who simply wants relationship with us.

This means that next time you need love, patience, kindness, gentleness—you can look to Jesus. It's not something you have to crank out on your own. He's our source for everything.

I'm not talking about "putting Jesus first." No, this is better than that. Jesus is not an item on your list. It's not "Jesus, family, work, golf, etc." He is life to us in the midst of all that we do in this life. He's active and present in all the activities of our lives. We don't do our daily "Jesus time" in the morning and then leave Him with our coffee as we go to work and love our family. No. Those things are the context by which we experience the indwelling life of Christ. A good laugh, a meal, an activity with friends, a long talk with a spouse, everyday work, class—we can experience Christ in all of these things.

Paul puts it this way: "When Christ, who is our life..." (Colossians 3:4). He's not merely someone we follow as He walks out ahead of us. No, He is everything to us. He's in us and united to us, and we don't know when He starts and where we end. We are that fused with Him.

Salvation is not merely a ticket to heaven one day. At salvation, we have been given eternal life. And eternal life isn't just life after death. Eternal life is Christ's own life in us (1 John 5:11–12). Further, Jesus tells us that eternal life is about knowing Him: "This is eternal life, that they may know You, the only true God, and Jesus Christ whom You have sent" (John 17:3).

Jesus died and was resurrected to give us eternal life—His life—in order for us to spend eternity simply knowing Him. That is the goal of the Christian life, to know Him. And since He's our life, we get to know Him more in every circumstance and activity of this life.

Jesus promises us an abundant life (John 10:10). But this abundant life is not better circumstances or a nicer house. The abundant life is Christ in us every single moment of every single day. We have all of Jesus in every moment. Since He's our life, not our changing circumstances or emotions, we can experience His abundance everywhere we go. His abundant joy and peace and love are ours, every moment.

In Philippians 3:8, Paul considered everything rubbish next to knowing Christ: "I consider everything a loss compared to the surpassing greatness of knowing Christ Jesus my Lord." It's that simple. God wants you to just know Him. It's so easy to turn our relationship with Christ into a job. We think, *Better do my good works and go to church and give my money.* And before we know it, it feels more like a membership than a relationship. Or a job than a romance. Yes, good works matter and serving matters and giving matters. But the fruit of knowing Jesus is that we will do all those things. Our only focus needs to be on knowing Him.

Knowing Christ as our life means knowing that Christ lives in us and we live in Him. These have been dominant themes in this book because they're the most dominant themes in the New Testament. "Christ lives in me" (Galatians 2:20). No matter the circumstance, no matter the pain or problem or concern, Christ lives in you. All the time. 24/7/365. We will spend eternity seeking to understand what it means for Christ to live in us.

Knowing Christ means enjoying the Person of Christ. We're commanded throughout Scripture to rejoice in God or delight in God or be glad in the Lord. And we do this because He is delighting in us. Enjoying Christ means soaking in His love and care for us. We're in our Father's hand. He cherishes us and loves us and longs for us to enjoy Him, His creation, and the good gifts He's given us.

"Christ in you" means you're not living the Christian life alone. You don't have to depend on your strength or your wisdom or your guidance; you have Christ in you living His life through you. This isn't passivity. And this isn't just Christ living. We are living and He is living. It's union with Christ. As we trust Him, He lives through us. And this means He uses our personality to express His love and life to the world.

I'm not saying, "It needs to be all of Christ and none of me." People quote John 3:30 as if it's a badge of humility. But think about it. We are the hands and feet of Jesus. We are His "instruments of righteousness" (Romans 6:13). He wants to use us, not eliminate us. He wants all of us, not less of us. We are not in His way. In context, John the Baptist was talking about his ministry getting out of the way so that Jesus could be the focus.

You're a brand-new creation! Jesus loves all of you and wants to use all of you! He wants the world to see Him in you. Biblical humility is saying the same thing God says about us. God doesn't want us to become smaller; that doesn't honor Him. What honors Him is when we give our entire selves to Him as living sacrifices to be used (Romans 12:1). You're the new self. You're holy, righteous, and acceptable to God. He likes you and loves everything about you.

Better Than the Old

The relationship we have with Christ is better than David's, Adam's, or any other Old Testament character's. David prayed that God wouldn't remove His Spirit and presence from Him (Psalm 51:11); God promises us that we are sealed by the Holy Spirit and He will never forsake us (Ephesians 1:13; Hebrews 13:5). David prayed for a clean heart and to be cleansed from sin (Psalm 51:2, 10); in Christ, we are forgiven and cleansed forever (Hebrews 10:10, 14; Colossians 2:13). And God has given us a new, pure heart (Matthew 5:8; Romans 6:17; 1 Timothy 1:5; Hebrews 10:22; Ezekiel 36:26). God has written His desires and instructions on our heart so that we now desire what He desires (Hebrews 8:10; Philippians 2:13).

God did more than just restore us back to relationship with Him. He gave us His life. Adam sinned and lost life. We sin every day and *never* lose life.[52] Why is that? Because we are in union with Christ and because God has forgiven us of our sins. We have something better than Adam: we have Christ as our life. Christ in us, our hope of glory! Sure, Adam walked *with* God. But in Christ, God lives *in* us fully (Colossians 2:9–10). We will be saved as long as Jesus lives, not as long as we live right (Hebrews 7:25). That is why our relationship with Him is better than even Adam's was!

Under the Old Covenant, everybody was constantly reminded of their sins (see Hebrews 10:3). But in our relationship with Christ under the New Covenant, God remembers our sins no more (Hebrews 10:17). Under the Old Covenant, God's presence was housed in the Holy of Holies in the temple, and only one person every year could enter God's presence. But in the New Covenant, we are the temple of God (1 Corinthians 6:19). We have access to God every single moment (Ephesians 3:12).

Under the Old Covenant, God blessed the people if they were faithful and cursed them if they weren't (Deuteronomy 28:1–68). Under the New Covenant, we are blessed with every spiritual blessing because Jesus became a curse for us (Ephesians 1:3; Galatians 3:13). Under the Old Covenant, God often grew angry with Israel and others (1 Kings 11:9; Psalm 78:59). But under the New Covenant, God promises to never grow angry with us because of what Christ has done for us (Isaiah 54:9; Romans 5:1). Under the Old Covenant, God would often turn away from Israel because of their sins and unfaithfulness (Acts 7:42; 2 Kings 17:23), and no one could see God or look at His face and live (Exodus 33:20). But under the New Covenant, God's eyes are always toward us, He lives in us, and He promises to be faithful even when we're unfaithful (1 Peter 3:12; Galatians 2:20; 2 Timothy 2:13). Under the Old Covenant, Moses begged for God's glory (Exodus 33:18). Under the New Covenant, God's glory is given to us freely, as a gift (John 17:22).

Whether it was Abraham or Jacob or Moses or Gideon, what we have is better than what they had. Hebrews 11:39–40 says, "And all these, having gained approval through their faith, did not receive what was promised, because God had provided something better for us." That something better is the relationship we have with God in the New Covenant. We need to stop relating to God like we're David or Moses. We need to start relating to God on the basis of all that Christ has done. He's made us pure, right, and together with Him forever. We need to stop trying to earn those things and start living from all that we've been given.

Jesus is better than your circumstances because His acceptance, love, and faithfulness to you are not based on what you go through. They're constant, unshakeable, and unbreakable because of His promise to you. He's life to you, even at your worst. He's for you, no matter what you feel day to day. He has set you free, He promises to continue setting you free, and He is always in you fighting for you to believe in His goodness and grace in the midst of all that you face each day.

EPILOGUE

Jesus really is this good. He truly is better. The gospel really is good news. Now, our journey of discovering the evidence for God, the reality of the New Covenant, and all that it means for Christ to live in us, may cause us to wonder, *What now?*

Whenever you go on vacation or receive a gift, you don't ask, "How do I apply this?" You simply give thanks and enjoy it. God wants us to enjoy Him while He enjoys us.

As I've taken this journey of discovering that Jesus is really this good, I've done more unlearning than learning. My hope and prayer for you is that as you continue trusting Jesus, you will begin to see everything in light of the cross and resurrection. That is our foundation.

In my relationship with my wife, Grace doesn't have to constantly lecture me about taking her to dinner or doing things for her. I do them because I love her and because she loves me. It's not a "duty" for me, it's a delight. I don't serve and love her out of fear or obligation. I do it because of the relationship I have with her. The same is true of Jesus.

Many people are scared of God's love and grace. They think it will lead to chaos or passivity or sin. But I've personally seen these truths revolutionize my life and the lives of hundreds of others. Every time, it only leads to loving God more. Paul knew God's grace, and this is what happened: "But by the grace of God I am what I am, and His grace toward me did not prove vain; but I labored even more than all of them, yet not I, but the grace of God with me" (1 Corinthians 15:10). He defined himself by God's grace, not his sin or performance. It was God's grace that enabled him to do more, not less. When our focus is on Jesus and not on what we're doing for Jesus, we end up doing more, not less.

As we conclude, I want to leave you with some passages I constantly come back to during times of doubt and struggle. God has forgiven you perfectly, forever. Read these slowly. You're perfected—not perfectly behaved, but perfectly forgiven and cleansed for all time. He's forgiven you of all—past, present, and future—sins:

> "For by one offering He has perfected for all time those who are sanctified." (Hebrews 10:14)

> "He made you alive together with Him, having forgiven us all our transgressions." (Colossians 2:13)

> "For I will be merciful to their iniquities, and I will remember their sins no more." (Hebrews 8:12)

You are safe and secure in Christ. Even at your worst, God still loves you and adores you and wants you and will always keep you:

> "No one is able to snatch them out of the Father's hand." (John 10:29)

> "I will never desert you, nor will I ever forsake you." (Hebrews 13:5)

> "He is able also to save forever those who draw near to God through Him." (Hebrews 7:25)

> "Now to him who is able to keep you from stumbling and to present you blameless before the presence of his glory with great joy." (Jude 24)

God's love for you is constant. His faithfulness to you is unchanging. No matter what you go through in this life, you can know that He is for you and not against you:

> "For I am convinced that neither death, nor life, nor angels, nor principalities, nor things present, nor things to come, nor powers, nor height, nor depth, nor any other created thing, will be able to separate us from the love of God, which is in Christ Jesus our Lord." (Romans 8:38–39)

> "If we are faithless, He remains faithful, for He cannot deny Himself." (2 Timothy 2:13)

> "What then shall we say to these things? If God is for us, who is against us?" (Romans 8:31)

You are a new creation, no matter what you feel, think, or do. You're a saint who sins. You're a child of God who is holy and righteous in Christ. That's who you are. And God is teaching you every day how to live out of who you are. He's not asking you to fake it. He's not asking you to be holy when you're really not. He's saying live godly because He's made you godly. He's not looking at you "as if you're righteous." You really are all that He says you are:

> "He made Him who knew no sin to be sin on our behalf, so that we might become the righteousness of God in Him." (2 Corinthians 5:21)

> "Through the obedience of the One the many will be made righteous." (Romans 5:19)

> "Therefore if anyone is in Christ, he is a new creature." (2 Corinthians 5:17)

> "In Him you have been made complete." (Colossians 2:10)

"So, as those who have been chosen of God, holy and beloved." (Colossians 3:12)

"Such were some of you; but you were washed, but you were sanctified, but you were justified in the name of the Lord Jesus Christ and in the Spirit of our God." (1 Corinthians 6:11)

"By this will we have been sanctified through the offering of the body of Jesus Christ once for all." (Hebrews 10:10)

"Seeing that His divine power has granted to us everything pertaining to life and godliness, through the true knowledge of Him who called us by His own glory and excellence. For by these He has granted to us His precious and magnificent promises, so that by them you may become partakers of the divine nature, having escaped the corruption that is in the world by lust." (2 Peter 1:3–4)

You don't have a wicked heart. Your heart is new, obedient, and full of God's love. You actually desire what God desires. That's why sin is no longer fulfilling for you:

"You became obedient from the heart to that form of teaching to which you were committed." (Romans 6:17)

"The love of God has been poured out within our hearts through the Holy Spirit who was given to us." (Romans 5:5)

"But as slaves of Christ, doing the will of God from the heart." (Ephesians 6:6)

"Moreover, I will give you a new heart and put a new spirit within you; and I will remove the heart of stone from your flesh and give you a heart of flesh." (Ezekiel 36:26)

God will never punish you or condemn you, ever. The cross dealt with that once and for all. You can have confidence on the day of judgment because He has taken away your sin:

> "By this, love is perfected with us, so that we may have confidence in the day of judgment; because as He is, so also are we in this world. There is no fear in love; but perfect love casts out fear, because fear involves punishment, and the one who fears is not perfected in love." (1 John 4:17–18)

> "Therefore there is now no condemnation for those who are in Christ Jesus." (Romans 8:1)

> "So Christ also, having been offered once to bear the sins of many, will appear a second time for salvation without reference to sin, to those who eagerly await Him." (Hebrews 9:28)

> "Therefore, having been justified by faith, we have peace with God through our Lord Jesus Christ." (Romans 5:1)

Christ is in you and you are in Christ. No matter what you go through in life, perhaps this is the most important thing you can remember. That is your defining point. You are enough and cherished and wanted and loved because you are in Christ and Christ is in you:

> "God willed to make known what is the riches of the glory of this mystery among the Gentiles, which is *Christ in you*, the hope of glory." (Colossians 1:27)

> "I have been crucified with Christ; and it is no longer I who live, but Christ lives in me; and the life which I now live in the flesh I live by faith in the Son of God, who loved me and gave Himself up for me." (Galatians 2:20)

> "But the one who joins himself to the Lord is *one spirit with Him*." (1 Corinthians 6:17)

"For you have died and your life is *hidden with Christ* in God." (Colossians 3:3)

"However, you are not in the flesh but *in the Spirit*, if indeed the Spirit of God dwells in you. But if anyone does not have the Spirit of Christ, he does not belong to Him." (Romans 8:9)

"For He rescued us from the domain of darkness, and transferred us to the kingdom of His beloved Son." (Colossians 1:13)

My prayer for you is the same prayer that Paul prayed to the Ephesians thousands of years ago. That you would come to understand how much God loves you. That your life would be rooted and grounded in His love for you. That you would realize His heart beats for you and He's in your heart, forever. And that you would live from His fullness and let Him do in you and through you more than you could ever ask or imagine:

"That He would grant you, according to the riches of His glory, to be strengthened with power through His Spirit in the inner man, so that Christ may dwell in your hearts through faith; and that you, being rooted and grounded in love, may be able to comprehend with all the saints what is the breadth and length and height and depth, and to know the love of Christ which surpasses knowledge, that you may be filled up to all the fullness of God. Now to Him who is able to do far more abundantly beyond all that we ask or think, according to the power that works within us." (Ephesians 3:16–20)

DID YOU ENJOY THIS BOOK?

If so, please leave a review on Amazon. This will help the book reach more people.

Also, you can give this book to a friend or order some more to give away. If you'd like to order more than twenty copies, please reach out to Zach for a bulk discount: Zach@ZachMaldonado.com

If you'd like Zach to come speak to your church, camp, group, or event, you can email him: Zach@ZachMaldonado.com

Zach created a free *Jesus Is Better* seven-part video study guide for you and your church or group. Go to ZachMaldonado.com to download the guide and access the videos.

Zach Maldonado serves as the community pastor at Church Without Religion in Lubbock, Texas. Zach is also the author of *The Cross Worked* and *Perfect and Forgiven*. He speaks at churches and events all over the United States and has a passion to proclaim the New Covenant message of God's grace.

Zach is happily married to his wife, Grace, and being her husband is his favorite thing in the world.

He holds a Master of Arts in Theology from Fuller Theological Seminary. You can connect personally with Zach on Instagram, Twitter, and Facebook (@ZachMaldo). You can also listen to his podcast, *The Daily Devotional Podcast*, anywhere you listen. If you have a question or just want to chat, you can email him at: Zach@ZachMaldonado.com.

ENDNOTES

1 Dominic Done, *When Faith Fails: Finding God in the Shadow of Doubt* (Nashville: Nelson Books, 2019).

2 Barna Group, "American Worldview Inventory 2020 – At a Glance," August 4, 2020, https://www.arizonachristian.edu/wp-content/uploads/2020/08/AWVI-2020-Release-08-Perceptions-of-Sin-and-Salvation.pdf.

3 Barna Group, "New Data on Gen Z – Perceptions of Pressure, Anxiety and Empowerment, February 1, 2021, https://www.barna.com/research/gen-z-success/.

4 Barna Group, "American Worldview Inventory 2020 – At a Glance," April 21, 2020, https://www.arizonachristian.edu/wp-content/uploads/2020/04/CRC-AWVI-2020-Release-03_Perceptions-of-God.pdf.

5 Robert Jastrow, *God and the Astronomers* (Toronto: W.W. Norton, 1992), 21.

6 Norman L. Geisler and Frank Turek, *I Don't Have Enough Faith to Be an Atheist* (Wheaton, IL: Crossway, 2004).

7 Stephen Hawking and Roger Penrose, *The Nature of Space and Time: The Isaac Newton Institute Series of Lectures* (Princeton, NJ: Princeton University Press, 1996), 20.

8 Richard Dawkins, *The God Delusion* (New York: Mariner, 2008), 168; Geisler and Turek, 78; William Lane Craig, *Reasonable Faith: Christian Truth and Apologetics* (Wheaton, IL: Crossway, 2008), 134–136.

9 Stephen W. Hawking, *A Brief History of Time* (New York: Bantam, 1988), 136–139. See also Norman Geisler and Peter Bocchino, *Unshakable Foundations* (Minneapolis: Bethany House, 2001), 107–110.

10 Geisler and Turek, 9.

11 David Barboza, "An iPhone's Journey, from the Factory Floor to the Retail Store," *New York Times*, https://www.nytimes.com/2016/12/29/technology/iphone-china-apple-stores.html#:~:text=There%20are%2094%20production%20lines,or%20roughly%20350%20a%20minute.

[12] Ibid., 98–104.

[13] Lee Strobel, *The Case for a Creator* (Grand Rapids, MI: Zondervan, 2009), 134.

[14] Hugh Ross, *Why I Believe in Divine Creation*, 138–141.

[15] Bart D. Ehrman, Did Jesus Exist? (New York: HarperOne, 2012), 5–6.

[16] The ten non-Christian sources are: Josephus; Tacitus, the Roman historian; Pliny the Younger, a Roman politician; Phlegon, a freed slave who wrote histories; Thallus, a first-century historian; Seutonius, a Roman historian; Lucian, a Greek satirist; Celsus, a Roman philosopher; Mara Bar-Serapion, a private citizen who wrote to his son; and the Jewish Talmud. For a complete listing of mentions of Christ from these sources, see Norman L. Geisler, *Baker Encyclopedia of Christian Apologetics* (Grand Rapids, MI: Baker Books, 1999), 381–385; see also Gary Habermas, *The Historical Jesus* (Joplin, MO: College Press, 1996), chapter 9.

[17] Geisler and Turek, 221–223.

[18] William D. Edwards, Wesley J. Gabel, and Floyd E. Hosmer, "On the Physical Death of Jesus Christ," *Journal of the American Medical Association*, March 21, 1986, 256.

[19] John Lennox, *Can Science Explain Everything?* (The Good Book Company, 2019).

[20] Ibid., 3.

[21] F. F. Bruce, *The Canon of Scripture* (Downers Grove, IL: IVP Academic, 2018). Craig L. Bloomberg, *The Historical Reliability of the Gospels* (Downers Grove, IL: IVP Academic, 2014). Josh McDowell, *The New Evidence that Demands a Verdict* (Nashville: Thomas Nelson, 1989), 36–37.

[22] Nelson Glueck, *Rivers in the Desert: A History of the Negev* (New York: Farrar, Strauss & Cudahy, 1959), 31.

[23] Josh McDowell, *The New Evidence that Demands a Verdict* (Nashville: Thomas Nelson, 1999). Titus Kennedy, *Unearthing the Bible* (Eugene, OR: Harvest House, 2020).

[24] Norman Geisler and Thomas Howe, *When Critics Ask* (Wheaton, IL: Victor, 1992), 385.

[25] William Ramsay, *St. Paul the Traveller and the Roman Citizen* (New York: Putnam, 1896), 8.

[26] Ibid., 34.

[27] Geisler and Turek, 225.

[28] Geisler, *Baker Encyclopedia of Christian Apologetics*, 532.

[29] As quoted in J. Ed Komoszewski, M. James Sawyer, Daniel B. Wallace, *Reinventing Jesus* (Grand Rapids, MI: Kregel, 2006), 215.

[30] Josh McDowell, *More Than a Carpenter* (Carol Stream, IL: Tyndale, 2004), 76.

[31] "Perceptions of Truth," Arizona Christian University, https://www.arizonachristian.edu/wp-content/uploads/2020/05/AWVI-2020-Release-05-Perceptions-of-Truth.pdf.

[32] Ibid., 1.

[33] C. S. Lewis, *Mere Christianity* (New York: MacMillan, 1952), 45.

[34] Paul Capon, *Is God A Moral Monster? Making Sense of the Old Testament God* (Grand Rapids: Baker Books, 2011), 173.

[35] Ibid., 175.

[36] Christopher J. H. Wright, *The God I Don't Understand: Reflections on Tough Questions of Faith* (Grand Rapids: Zondervan, 2008), 88.

[37] Capon, 180.

[38] Ibid., 181–182.

[39] Ibid., 182–184.

[40] "What Was Jesus' View of the Old Testament?" Blue Letter Bible, https://www.blueletterbible.org/Comm/stewart_don/faq/bible-authoritative-word/question17-jesus-view-of-the-old-testament.cfm.

[41] "Harris Poll Survey of American Happiness," https://theharrispoll.com/heres-how-happy-americans-are-right-now/.

[42] "What Is the Science of Happiness?" *Berkeley Wellness,* November 9, 2015, http://www.berkeleywellness.com/healthy-mind/mind-body/article/what-science-happiness.

[43] "Research," Back to the Bible, https://www.backtothebible.org/research.

[44] "American Piety in the 21st Century," Baylor University, https://www.baylor.edu/baylorreligionsurvey/doc.php/288937.pdf.

[45] Barna Group, "The Connected Generation," https://theconnectedgeneration.com/.

[46] The word *flesh* is the old way we used to think and act that's still leftover. All of our habits and old thinking didn't disappear when we came to Christ (see. Philippians 3:4-6; 1 Corinthians 1:26; Romans 8:6–7; Galatians 5:16–17; 2 Corinthians 10:3; Galatians 3:3).

[47] I learned this concept from Andrew Farley in I(Grand Rapids, MI: Zondervan, 2009), 97.

[48] John Lynch, *The Cure*: CrossSection, 2011), 37.

[49] Lucas S. LaFreniere and Michelle G. Newman, "Exposing Worry's Deceit: Percentage of Untrue Worries in Generalized Anxiety Disorder Treatment," Science Direct, https://www.sciencedirect.com/science/article/abs/pii/S0005789419300826. Robert Leahy in his book, "The Worry Cure," cites a study that showed 85 percent of what people worried about didn't

happen. Robert Leahy, *The Worry Cure: Seven Steps to Stop Worry from Stopping You* (New York: Three Rivers Press, 2005).

[50] Joshua Brown and Joel Wong, "How Gratitude Changes You and Your Brain," *Greater Good Magazine*, June 6, 2017, https://greatergood.berkeley.edu/article/item/how_gratitude_changes_you_and_your_brain.

[51] See N. T. Wright, *The Climax of the Covenant* (Minneapolis: Fortress, 1991), 181; Douglas Moo, *Five Views on Law and Gospel* (Counterpoints: Bible and Theology) (Grand Rapids, MI: Zondervan, 2010), 375–376; and Tom Schriener: https://www.thegospelcoalition.org/article/old-covenant-response-andy-stanley/.

[52] This insight came through conversations and teaching from Andrew Farley.